Vibrations
making unorthodox musical instruments

THE RESOURCES OF MUSIC SERIES
General Editors: *Wilfrid Mellors, John Paynter*

THE RESOURCES OF MUSIC *by Wilfrid Mellers*
SOUND AND SILENCE *by John Paynter and Peter Aston*
SOMETHING TO PLAY *by Geoffrey Brace*
MUSIC DRAMA IN SCHOOLS *edited by Malcolm John*
THE PAINFUL PLOUGH *by Roy Palmer*
THE VALIANT SAILOR *by Roy Palmer*
TROUBADOURS *by Brian Sargent*
MINSTRELS *by Brian Sargent*
POVERTY KNOCK *by Roy Palmer*
THE RIGS OF THE FAIR *by Roy Palmer and Jon Raven*
JAZZ *by Graham Collier*
POP MUSIC IN SCHOOL *edited by Graham Vulliamy and Ed Lee*
FOLK MUSIC IN SCHOOL *edited by Robert Leach and Roy Palmer*
VIBRATIONS *by David Sawyer*
MINSTRELS 2 *by Brian Sargent*

RECORDINGS

SOUND AND SILENCE – record *John Paynter and Peter Aston*
TROUBADOURS AND MINSTRELS – record *Brian Sargent*
JAZZ: ILLUSTRATIONS - record *Graham Collier*
JAZZ: RHYTHM SECTION – tape *Graham Collier*
JAZZ: LECTURE CONCERT – record *Graham Collier*
POP MUSIC IN SCHOOL – tape *Graham Vulliamy and Ed Lee*

Vibrations

making unorthodox musical instruments

DAVID SAWYER

CAMBRIDGE UNIVERSITY PRESS
Cambridge
London · New York · Melbourne

Published by the Syndics of the Cambridge University Press
The Pitt Building, Trumpington Street, Cambridge CB2 1RP
Bentley House, 200 Euston Road, London NW1 2DB
32 East 57th Street, New York, NY 10022, USA
296 Beaconsfield Parade, Middle Park, Melbourne 3206, Australia

© Cambridge University Press 1977

First published 1977
Reprinted 1979

Drawings by Ted Draper

Printed in Great Britain at the
University Press, Cambridge

Library of Congress Cataloguing in Publication Data

Sawyer, David.
Vibrations.
(The Resources of music series)
1. Musical instruments — Construction. I. Title.
II. Series.
ML460.S27   781.9'1   76-11499
ISBN 0 521 20812 2

Contents

To Caspar

Introduction

I began making unorthodox musical instruments in 1966 whilst a student at Exeter College of Art. At that time, part of the fine art course required that I execute pieces of sculpture. I was unable to convince myself that making three-dimensional *objets d'art* was a worthwhile activity so I began to think about 'making' which would result in an object with a function, free of aesthetic concerns. Previous study in architecture had taught me a little about basic design and how to work from a brief. All I needed was the brief.

Music had always meant a lot to me and at that time I possessed a recorder, concert flute and alto saxophone. I was highly influenced by the classics but felt no urge to perform them. The instruments I owned, I played for my own amusement and occasionally with fellow musicians.

I knew that I wanted to make music and became attracted to jazz, but whether from a basic lack of confidence in my playing ability or dissatisfaction with the traditional chord progressions inherent in jazz, I remained unhappy about how best to express myself musically.

At about this time, parallel to my college studies, I was occasionally teaching art at a local psychotherapy centre. Some of the patients were interested in music-making, so we arranged some sessions using an assortment of instruments from the centre and simple percussion instruments I had bought recently. The music was bizarre. Everybody seemed to be following his own train of musical thought without there being any central theme to which players adhered. Playing without printed music came quite naturally to me as I had never been interested in sight-reading. I learnt the recorder at secondary school and, apart from playing some basic compositions as exercises, found enjoyment in inventing my own tunes. But this approach, practised by four or five players, immediately struck me as very confusing. As an activity it was full of surprises, but I could not see where it was leading. Nevertheless, the sum-total of these interests led me to begin making my own musical instruments.

I started by reading a book called *Musical Instruments made to be Played* by Ronald Roberts, and various others on the physics of sound and on scientific studies of musical instruments. I also studied books on musical instruments from different parts of the world and found that I was most interested in primitive instruments that still retained the look of the original material. Thus bamboo was of immediate interest and next the gourd, coconut and the tin can which, although not in the same class as the preceding materials, has, like them, built-in acoustic properties.

My first instruments remained close to tradition, but with success I ventured into designs which required building the whole object, instead of relying on the ready-made forms mentioned above.

I retained both methods of design, experimenting in the three main sound areas of wind, string and percussion, and those areas which are not so easily described, to which the Jew's harp belongs. At this stage I had no clear idea where the process was leading, although I continued to find satisfaction in discovering new sounds by exploring the acoustic nature of materials ranging through wood, metal, clay, plastic, cloth and paper.

As I was fundamentally involved in sound, and was not designing the instruments to be capable of making a particular kind of music (apart from one or two flutes tuned to a major scale and a tin fiddle with frets tuned chromatically), I assumed that they should either be used rhythmically or merely for sound effects. But at the same time, listening to music of India, Bali, Japan and Africa caused me to re-examine my musical values, which were somewhat entrenched in Western tradition; while the music and instruments of Harry Partch showed me that even new scales could be invented and, together with the new instruments of the Baschet brothers, reassured me of the relevance of my own work.

Since Western music became an art-form it has been continually changing, and possibly its most dramatic development was initiated by Schoenberg. Avant-garde music and jazz take full advantage of atonality, but I have avoided the former because of its academic foundations, and the latter because of its tradition.

My first uncontrolled music sessions haunted me enough to arrange others with fellow musicians. These became improvisations, loosely structured around rhythms and repeated passages that evolved as we played. I also arranged sessions in which only my own instruments were used. The sound was quite different, but the rhythms and repeated passages persisted.

I had begun to use my instruments in the theatre, where the musical requirements were governed by a script. Here the sounds had an obvious function and music *per se* was not essential. But a music which would explore the full potential of my instruments still remained elusive. I next began running courses on experimental musical instrument making, often concluding with a musical perform-ance, mostly by non-musicians. A new approach to music-making was developing, although I was still too unsure of my ground to put complete faith in the process.

So I began employing simple number systems in audience-participation sessions, in which the players chose from a selection of my instruments. The activity was absorbing and resulted in complex sound patterns, but it limited personal exploration.

I had, on occasions, composed for conventional instruments but found the process arduous and essentially egocentric, reducing the musicians to mere technicians. I also realised that to compose for my own instruments, many of which had unrelated scales, was going to bring them in line with conventional methods.

Only through a break with orthodox thinking was I able to conceive an idea which gave considerably more scope to the instruments and players. This necessitated abandoning all musical judgement and procedure, including emotive aims.

I realised that inviting the audience to participate in a performance was a way of avoiding the full confrontation with the public that normally occurs. Although this had proved a worthwhile experience, in the light of my new thinking, it was clearly a device to hide my own lack of confidence as a performer. The acid test was to perform publicly. As my collection contained over fifty instruments, I decided that at least four or five players would be necessary to do justice to the full range during a concert, and that the players would not rehearse, as I believed that whatever happened during a performance was an integral part of that performance. For want of a better word, the music was described as 'improvisation', although no theme was even remotely considered. Nevertheless, some musical material, mainly rhythmic, arose more or less spontaneously and seemed to lure players towards a traditional unity.

After two performances, the group took the name 'Impulse', and 'improvisation' became a redundant term as our new title led us to consider spontaneity to be the essence of a performance. Those first sessions at the psychotherapy centre no longer seemed bizarre, as spontaneity had clearly played a major role: but as the subject was now in the open, our concept of the word would have to be investigated. This became no mean task.

Having made sound and video recordings of some concerts we were able to study performances. It became apparent that we were not making a clean break with tradition and that to do so would require a special awareness to recognise when memory was dictating. Examples of this use of memory were rhythms, including repeated passages, and conscious phrasing. In other words, composing, which was the right of every player, had to be thoroughly scrutinised. Technical competence, the assumed tool of musicians, which so easily becomes the means to composition would possibly need to be unlearned or, more practically speaking, to be discarded. On the other hand, performances must not become a kind of music therapy for the group. The task was indeed daunting. I realised the solution lay in the instruments themselves which, being unconventional, could guide us past our newly-discovered musical traps. The instruments were, in general, the outcome of acoustic concerns and subsequent use played no part in their design. But, in spite of this factor, various styles associated with conventional instruments had been used by the group from the begin-

11

ning and only by reversing the roles of player and instrument would we stop using them merely to express our emotions and begin to consider their fundamental qualities. In other words, the act of charming sounds from an instrument must completely dominate the player's own imagination. This mode of playing is a natural progression from the making of an instrument, which fundamentally entails designing and constructing materials to vibrate in a specific manner. At this point, the concern for spontaneity becomes irrelevant as the acts of making and playing emerge as a total process, unfettered by any musical connotations. This book is a practical manual which enters the domain of audible vibration: an essential path for musicians and non-musicians alike.

Materials and tools*

In my notes on musical instruments I refer to bamboo, coconuts, tins and an assortment of wood and small essential parts. Some parts, such as a violin peg and wire, are available from music shops. Other shops to consider for supplies are 'do-it-yourself' shops, craft shops and the hardware stores. A chemist or wine-making supplier will have rubber tube; model shops sell fine plastic fuel pipe. Your tins should be no problem and, in season, a greengrocer will have walnuts and coconuts. Buy fishing weights and nylon line from a sports shop and invisible nylon thread and cotton tape from a haberdasher. Bamboo is one of my favourite materials; long pieces are used to wrap carpets round, so a furnishing store may stock the bigger sizes. Smaller-diameter bamboo is carried by most garden shops, otherwise order your bamboo from: The Bamboo People, Godmanstone, Nr Dorchester, Dorset. This firm stocks and delivers bamboo in all dimensions up to 7.5 cm (and, occasionally, 10 cm) diameter.

My making takes place on our lounge carpet. Very infrequently I need power equipment and sometimes I use a firm table and a small wood vice. The tools include saws, files, pliers, scissors, drills, a pricker, screwdriver, countersinker, surforms, G-clamps, a Stanley knife, small sharp kitchen knife, hammer and soldering iron (60 W). The consumables are a selection of sandpapers, transparent sticky tape, varnish, glues, files and solder.

Saws: small hack-saw,
pad-saw,
coping-saw,
fret-saw.

Files: round files,
half-inch and quarter-inch, half-round and flat files (medium and
fine),
various needle files.

Drills: brace and bits (augers),
hand drill and twist drills,
small power drill and highspeed wood drills.

*Throughout the book, dimensions are given in a mixture of metric and imperial units, reflecting the gradual changeover to metric units. As metrication proceeds, items will appear in metric units which may not be the exact equivalent of those presently available in imperial units, necessitating some slight adjustments.

Surforms: round surform file,
               small flat surform file.

Glues: Evo-Stik Resin W, or equivalent, for wood to wood,
               Araldite for wood to metal.

Coconuts and bamboo are no problem to cut, although bamboo will split if gripped too tightly in a vice. Bamboo has an outside skin, in some ways equivalent to bark, which will tear easily. To avoid damaging the surface, saw slowly right to the point where the saw cuts through the last strands of bamboo fibre. The wood is hard, but has a simple straight grain, so splitting lengths for a bamboo xylophone is a simple matter. If the outside skin has been damaged, the whole outer surface can be scraped off revealing a pale orange grain. This surface will take varnish. Figure 1 shows the detail of a piece of bamboo. The proportions and principles laid out in the instrument sections may serve as guidelines for further experimentation based on those particular designs. In other words, using the tin fiddle as an example, if you wish to make a larger fiddle, various components would need to be larger, including the tin, fret-board and thickness of the wire.

Sound ideas can also be developed using any objects which have acoustic properties. An object may be adapted to become part of an instrument, for example a paraffin can could be used for the sound box of a fretted instrument. The 'steel drum', initially an oil drum, has become Trinidad's national instrument.

As with all creative forms, possibilities exist wherever and whenever you and I can find our way into a primarily personal adventure. My process of working has always been experimental, so I would like to leave this book open-ended in the belief that the action of the individual will ultimately prevail.

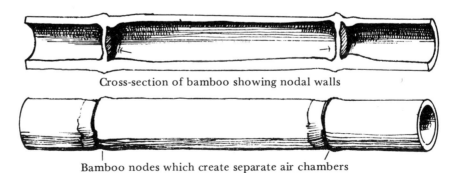

Cross-section of bamboo showing nodal walls

Bamboo nodes which create separate air chambers

Figure 1

Students performing with their own instruments

15

Bamboo slit drum

Initially I was fascinated by the wood block (figure 2). I made one from a piece of mahogany, and then made a small slit drum (figure 3) from a piece of fruit-wood. In both cases, wood had to be gouged out to create a cavity. I decided to experiment with bamboo because of its natural cavity. I was also interested in the 'teponaxtli' of Central America (figure 4), which has an H-shaped slit. I used this shape for a slot, but with the H repositioned.

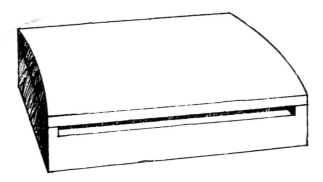

Figure 2. *Wood block*

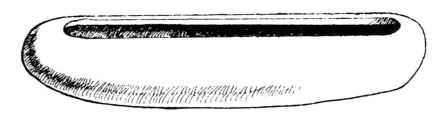

Figure 3. *Slit drum*

Description   Length 16 cm, average diameter 6 cm. The drum is a length of bamboo with a node (the natural division in bamboo) at both ends. Between the nodes are three slots in the form of a broad H producing two bamboo tongues.

Pitch*   C♯, 554.4 hertz.

*The pitch is obtained by comparison with standard tuning forks. The findings are included to represent the instruments more clearly.

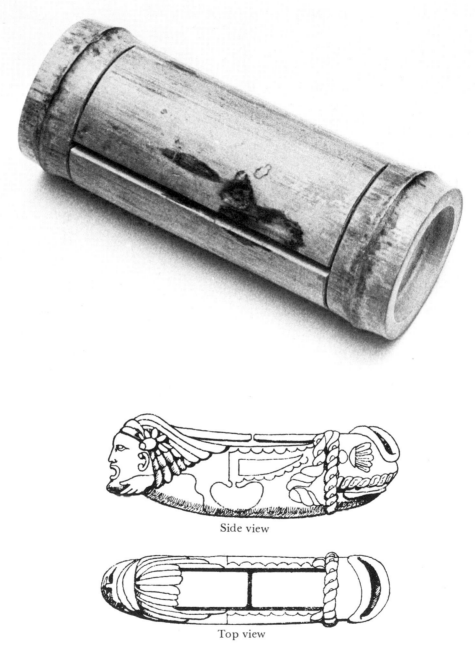

Side view

Top view

Figure 4. *Central American 'teponaxtli'*

Playing The instrument is played by holding it gently in the palm of one hand and striking with a soft beater, close to the centre bar of the H-form, where the two tongues meet.

17

Acoustics   The two tongues are cut equally so that they give the same note. For the instrument to sound true, the pitch of the tongues must be the same as that of the bamboo chamber. When one of the tongues is beaten, the vibration corresponds exactly with the natural wavelength of the chamber. The air in the cavity vibrates in sympathy with the tongue vibration, amplifying the note of the tongue.

Making   Using a fine-toothed saw, cut a length of bamboo to include two nodes, producing one closed chamber. Cut into the bamboo 1 cm in from each node, and parallel to the node (figure 5). If the two

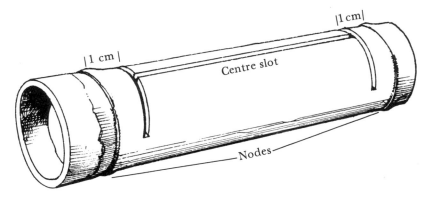

Figure 5

nodes are not parallel compromise by making the two saw-cuts parallel. At first the cuts should only just penetrate the chamber.

The lengthways slot must now be made. One way is to draw a line between the two cuts, and with a small pad-saw cut down the line, making the third slot. Another way of producing the third slot, is to drive a knife through the bamboo starting at the top cut, and forcing the wood to split along its grain until it reaches the second cut. This must be done carefully with a second person holding the bamboo upright on a firm surface. The blunt edge of the knife is tapped gently with a hammer, so that the blade does not penetrate beyond the second cut. Whichever way the third cut has been made, it must now be widened to approximately 5 mm to allow the tongues to vibrate freely. The easiest way is the knife method, above, removing thin lengths by splitting the bamboo. The slot can be finished with a fine hand-file. The effect of joining the two initial cuts with a third is to produce two wide short tongues.

The next and final stage is to tune the instrument. At this stage, the tongue note will be high in comparison with the cavity note. The pitch of the tongue can be found by beating the centre of its free end. The cavity note is less easily heard but, by blowing gently across the centre slot, the wind sound will carry a general pitch. The note of the tongues must now be lowered. This is done by lengthening the side slots equally on either side of the centre slot. As the tongues get longer, their pitch descends. During this process, regular comparison must be made between the tongues (which must always have the same pitch) and between the note of the tongues and that of the cavity. When the tongues and cavity are the same, the note will be strong and rich. If one or both tongues have too low a pitch, this can be raised by filing the free ends (this reduces the weight of a tongue and thus allows it to vibrate more rapidly).

Pitch tube

During a concert of percussion music I noticed some instruments called 'pieces of wood'. The pitch tube is a replica in bamboo. I have found no other reference to this instrument.

Description Large tube: length 42 cm, diameter 4.5 cm. Small tube: length 20 cm, diameter 3 cm. The tube is a length of bamboo without nodes. It has a rounded slot exactly half-way along it.

Pitch Large tube: D♯, 322.2 hertz. Small tube: D, 1174.8 hertz.

Playing The pitch tube is held loosely in the manner shown in figure 6, and struck firmly with a heavy wooden beater (a blackboard peg will do).

Acoustics The slot produces a point of weakness. Struck directly above that point, the tube bends up and down on either side. If the air in the tube responds to the same vibration rate, the wood note will be amplified making a pure note, the two pitches will act in sympathy.

Making Using a fine-toothed saw, cut a length of bamboo without nodes. This makes a hollow tube. Balance the piece on your finger and mark the point of balance. This is the place where the slot should be made.

Tap your finger across the top of the tube, the note produced is the pitch of the cavity. Tap the tube *near* the top. This will also give

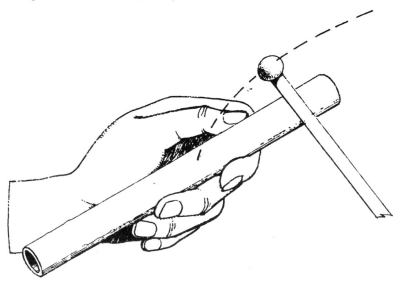

Figure 6. *Playing the pitch tube*

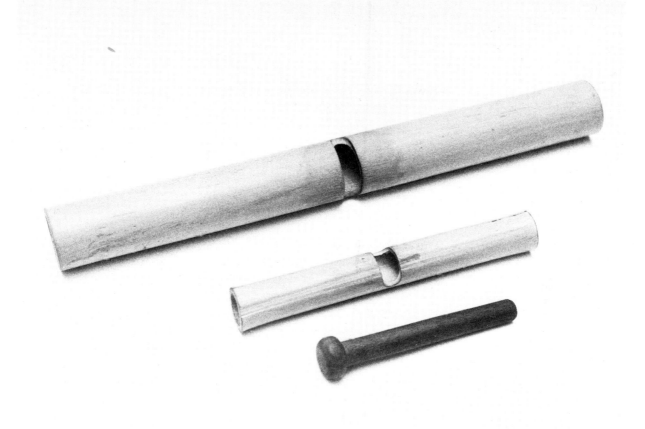

a note, higher in comparison (this is the pitch of the wood). The intention is to make the note of the cavity the same as that of the wood.

Use a half-inch round file to make the centre slot, filing carefully as bamboo skin tears easily. If it does tear, file smooth with a finer file. Keep the file at right angles to the bamboo. When the file cuts into the cavity, test the note of the cavity against that of the wood, as before. The former will have risen and the latter descended. Continue filing and testing until the two notes coincide.

Bamboo bonca

My first efforts were based on a hardwood percussion instrument (figure 7). I used the idea with bamboo but had no clear success until I experimented with the relationship between slot and cavity.

Figure 7

Description — Large bonca: length 31 cm, diameter 4.5 cm, slots 15 cm long. Small bonca: length 17 cm, diameter 4 cm approximately, slots 7.5 cm long. The slots in both examples are exactly opposite each other producing equally weighted tongues. The resonant cavity below the slots is closed by a node in the long bonca and open in the small bonca.

Pitch — Large bonca: A, 440 hertz. Small bonca: D, 1174.8 hertz.

Playing — Hold below the slots with one of the tongues facing upwards. Using a soft beater, strike close to the tongue end.

Acoustics — The bonca has tongues which work on the same basis as the tuning fork, but with a resonator attached. The resonator is the open or closed cavity below the tongues. A cavity sealed at one end acts like an organ pipe which is blocked at the top. The pitch is an octave lower than it would be if the tube were unstopped. In other words, to obtain the pitch of the longer bonca with an open tube, the resonator would have to be twice as long as it would when closed. Where the resonator is a hollow tube, the hand must not obstruct the opening in any way, as this will change the effective length of the tube, and therefore alter its relationship with the note of the tongue.

Making — Whichever bonca you are making, the tuning principle is the same. Mark two lines exactly opposite each other on the open end of either tube. On the unstopped tube, the choice is arbitrary. Continue these two lines down the sides of the bamboo. These are the guides for the saw cuts to make the tongues. Do not attempt to cut both at the same time, as the blade will rip the skin off the bamboo on the side furthest from the handle of the saw. Also, it is more accurate to cut along a line that you can see. Using a pad-saw, begin cutting into one side (figure 8). (With an unstopped tube, the slots extend slightly less than half-way down, with a stopped tube, the slots extend closer

22

Figure 8. *Detail of slot*

to half-way.) Do not let one slot become much longer than the other during cutting. When testing for pitch sympathy, make sure the two slots are of equal length.

The note of the wood is relatively easy to hear; that of the cavity is less distinct. With the open tube, blow across the end, and listen to the general pitch of the wind. With the stopped tube, blow across the base of the slot. As the slots are lengthened, the tongue pitch goes down and the cavity pitch rises. At one point, the two meet. If you go beyond this point, that is, if the tongue note becomes lower than that of the cavity, the tongues must be carefully shortened. An alternative method for a small change is to file the slot opening to widen it, effectively reducing the tongue weight, and raising its pitch.

23

Metal bonca

This instrument is a direct interpretation of the bamboo bonca into metal.

Description Large bonca: length 30 cm, slots 10.6 cm long. Small bonca: length 26 cm, slots 10 cm long. Both are made from square-section metal tube such as Dexion 'Speedframe' with 2.5 cm sides.

Pitch Large bonca: F♯, 740 hertz. Small bonca: G♯, 830.6 hertz.

Playing Using a soft beater, strike close to the tongue end, as with the bamboo bonca.

Acoustics The same principle applies as did with the bamboo bonca. Because the instrument is metal, the note rings for longer than wood. Upper harmonics are strongly present, giving the note a rich quality.

Making Draw two lines for saw-cut guides, down two opposite faces; make the cuts with an eclipse 66 saw (figure 9). Use the same method of tuning as for the bamboo bonca. So far I have experimented with bars between 24 and 45 cm long.

Figure 9. *Detail of slot*

Ratchet

This instrument is based on the football rattle (figure 10).

Description This instrument is a 32 cm length of bamboo with a node approximately 8 cm from one end, creating a handle. Beyond this division the bamboo is split to make two arms and a tongue. The two arms support the ratches wheel (a wooden ball, diameter 4.5 cm) and the tongue clicks against the wheel which revolves on a steel spindle (length 7 cm, diameter $\frac{1}{8}$ inch).

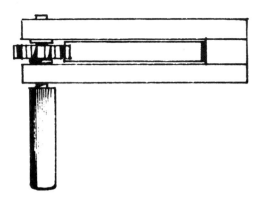

Figure 10. *Football rattle*

Pitch Indefinite.

Playing Hold in one hand, and rub the ratchet wheel on the palm of the other hand towards the fingers. For extended sounds the wheel can be rubbed on clothing., furniture, etc.

Acoustics The bamboo tongue repeatedly striking the ratchet teeth produces a high sharp 'ratatat'. The fundamental note of the bamboo tongue is not audible.

Making Cut a piece of bamboo 2.5 cm in diameter, retaining one node 9 cm from one end (figure 11). Fit a jubilee clip firmly, close to the node on the longer shank. Mark eight equal divisions around the end of the long shank. The tongue will be two divisions wide, the arms are each three divisions wide. Using the knife splitting method (as described in the section on the bamboo slit drum), run three clefts down to the jubilee clip to make the tongue and two arms.

26

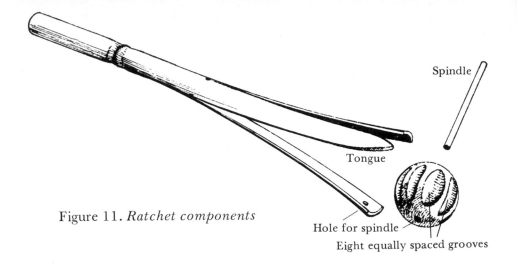

Figure 11. *Ratchet components*

Spindle

Tongue

Hole for spindle

Eight equally spaced grooves

Now the ratchet wheel can be made. A wooden ball is first drilled through its centre with an $\frac{1}{8}$ inch twist drill, so that it will revolve evenly on its spindle. On the ball draw eight equally spaced lines lengthways between the holes just made for the spindle. These are the positions of the grooves. File them out with a surform round file, cutting to half the depth of the file. Finish with a half-inch round file and sandpaper. Now drive the steel spindle through the wheel with approximately 1 cm of steel protruding at either side. Remove burrs. Next the bamboo arms must be steamed into an open position so that the fitted wheel can revolve freely. A piece of $\frac{1}{2}$ inch dowel 5 cm long can be used temporarily to keep the two arms apart. Position the dowel at the top end of the arms initially. Steaming can be done easily using a kettle with not too much water in it so that the steam comes mainly through the spout. The steaming and bending take place just above the jubilee clip. Hold the bamboo close to the spout for maximum effect, and be careful not to scald yourself. Steam for two minutes and then dowse in cold water to freeze it; remove the dowel. The arms will spring back to some degree. Now refit the dowel forcing the arms further apart, and begin steaming again. Continue this procedure until the arms stay apart long enough for the wheel to slot in. Ensure that the arms are steamed evenly. The $\frac{1}{8}$ inch holes to house the spindle must now be drilled. These are half-way across and 8 mm down from the top of each arm. Fit the wheel. It may rub on one side of each arm, but this excess bamboo should be cut off, filed away and sanded. Lastly, the bamboo tongue should be trimmed so that it strikes the oncoming teeth cleanly. In the example shown, the end of the tongue was removed to ensure a single point of contact with the teeth. If the tongue is pressing too hard, or not hard enough, onto the teeth, it can be steamed to the correct angle. Likewise, if the arms have moved, a further steaming will help. The jubilee clip can now be removed. To discourage any further splitting, drill an $\frac{1}{8}$ inch hole just beyond the base of each slit as in figure 11. Using a flat fine needle file, file down the slits until they reach the holes. The tongue will now vibrate more freely.

Bamboo scraper

This instrument is often made with a slot running between two nodes (figure 12). It is far simpler to make a slot once the nodal ends are removed.

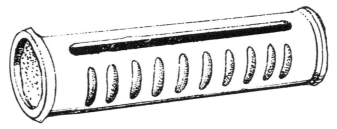

Figure 12

Description　Length 34 cm, diameter 4.5 cm. The scraper is a length of bamboo without nodes. A slit runs along the whole length of the instrument with a series of parallel grooves at right angles to it.

Pitch　Indefinite.

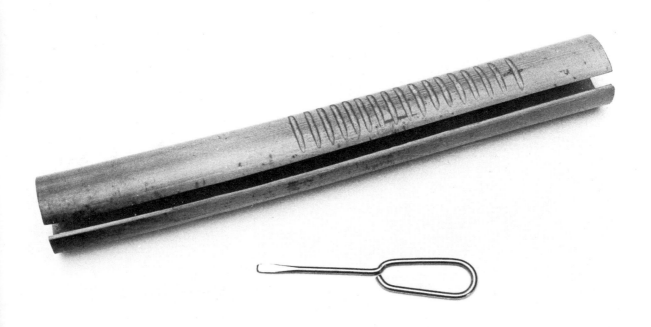

<dl>
<dt>Playing</dt>
<dd>Hold the instrument lightly in one hand, and run a screwdriver across the grooves.</dd>
</dl>

Acoustics　The tension in the bamboo is removed by cutting a slit down its length. The action of the screwdriver striking the groove edges causes the wood to vibrate and sound. Due to growth differences in the bamboo, each side may have a different sound.

Making　With a fine hack-saw, cut a length of bamboo without nodes, giving a hollow tube of bamboo. Make a lengthways slit using a knife and hammer. Drive the knife at right angles to the end, down through the tube, tapping the blunt edge of the knife gently. The blade will follow the grain. Using the same technique, remove a strip of bamboo to make the slit about 1 cm wide. File and sand to remove splinters and burrs. Using a quarter-inch round file, make a series of grooves along one or both sides of the slit. The grooves begin close to the slit and are approximately 3 cm in length. In the example shown they are set about 1 cm apart, but varying the positions of the grooves will create different sound patterns.

Bamboo claves

This instrument is a replica of the Japanese 'yotsu dake' (figure 13) split bamboo castanets.

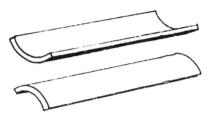

Figure 13. *Japanese 'yotsu dake'*

Description Both claves are 21 cm long and of equal thickness. They differ only in the degree of curvature.

Pitch F♯, 740 hertz and G♯, 830.6 hertz.

Playing The claves should be held as shown in figure 14. The more loosely the beater clave is held, the brighter the sound. The outer surfaces make contact, the beater striking its opposite along the middle of their curved surfaces. The claves can be changed around. A more precise note can be produced by using the edge of the beater to strike the curved surface of the second clave.

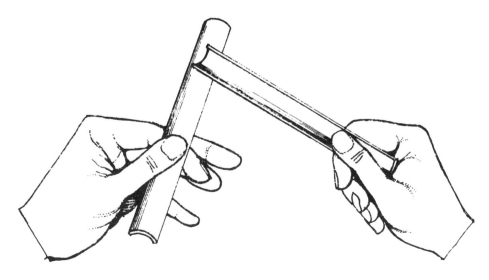

Figure 14. *Playing the bamboo claves*

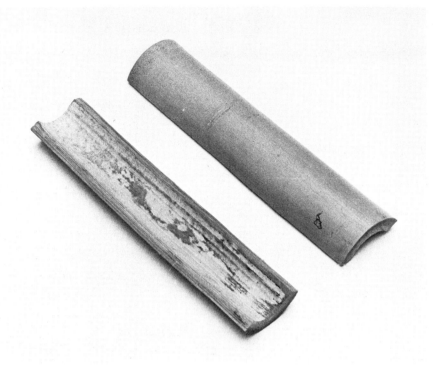

Acoustics   Each bar has a pitch, so when the two are struck together, two notes are heard. (Similarly, if two xylophone bars are struck together two notes will sound.)

Making   Take a length of bamboo without nodes (giving an open bamboo tube). Split the bamboo lengthways as described in the section on the bamboo scraper and split again to produce two bars. The positioning of the second split dictates the pitch of the two bars. Further pitch change of a bar is made by splitting off sections of bamboo. The effect is to lower the note.

33

Hand clapper

This instrument is an adaptation of the bamboo claves.

Description   Large: length 15 cm. Medium: length 4.5 cm. Small: length 1.4 cm. In each case, two approximately identical bamboo claves are tapped together down one side (figure 15).

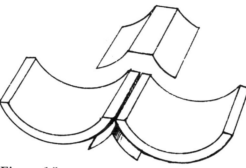

Figure 15

Pitch   Indefinite, but the larger the instrument the deeper the tone.

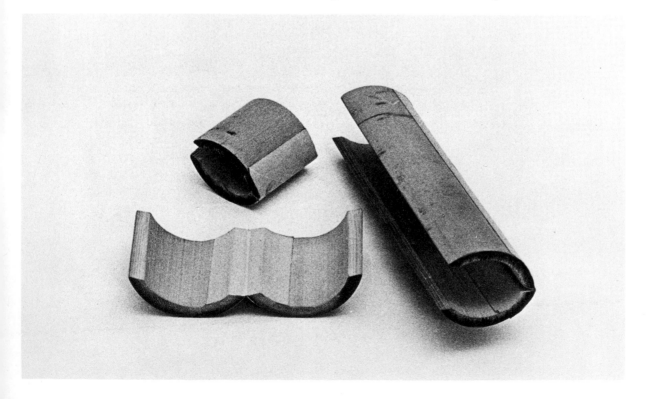

Playing   The clapper is laid in the palm of one hand, and tapped with the fingers of the other hand.

Acoustics The sound is similar to that of the bamboo claves, except that some of the vibrations are amplified in the enclosed space.

Making   As with the bamboo claves, two bars are needed. The two edges of each bar must be sanded so they fit together, making a flattened tube (lozenge shape in section). Hinge the two halves together with masking tape, or plastic sticky tape (PVC tape). Do the insides first making sure the edges touch. Tape the outside so that the two free edges spring slightly apart. Trim off excess tape.

Bamboo chime bar

This instrument is a straightforward version of the European metal chime bar (figure 16).

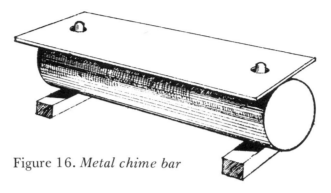

Figure 16. *Metal chime bar*

Description   This instrument consists of a section (or bar) of bamboo supported over a tube of bamboo with nodes at both ends which acts as a resonator. The bamboo section or bar is 43 cm long and the resonator is 48.5 cm long and 5 cm diameter. The opening half-way along the resonator is a round hole 2.5 cm diameter. The supports consist of $1\frac{1}{2}$ inch round wire 14 gauge nails with sleeves of 8 mm rubber piping and 5 mm model aircraft plastic fuel pipe. The foot is a 5 cm length of $\frac{1}{2}$ inch dowel with a piece of sponge draught excluder attached.

Pitch   C, 261.6 hertz.

Playing   The instrument should be placed on a soft surface and the bar struck directly above the hole in the resonator with a cork or soft beater.

Acoustics   The bar is supported at the two nodal points. These are the places of least movement when the bar is vibrating. The note produced is weak and must be amplified by a resonator. If the cavity has the same pitch as the bar, the chamber will vibrate in sympathy, thus amplifying the bar note.

Making bar   Bamboo poles are often split when bought, but are quite satisfactory for this part of the exercise. Using an eclipse hack-saw, cut a straight length of bamboo between two nodes. If the pole is not split, just cut between two nodes and split the tube lengthways with a knife. The greater the curvature of the bar, the more rigid and high-pitched the note will be. The less curved the bar, the more flexible and low-pitched the note will be. Tuning this part of the instrument is described later.

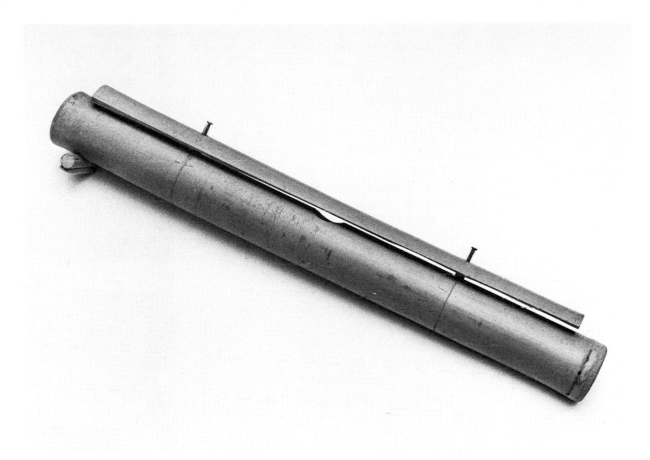

Making resonator Choose a length of bamboo which is not split between two nodes.
Cut the pole with a small hack-saw outside the two nodes to make a
single enclosed chamber. The longer and wider the tube, the deeper
its resonant pitch will be. A hole must be drilled into the chamber at
its centre. If the tube is smaller than the one shown, the hole can be
smaller, though no less than 2 cm in diameter, or the action of the
resonator will be reduced. If you are using a brace and bit, drill a
guide hole with a twist drill for the auger bit screw to slot in. Bamboo
splits very readily, so make sure that the centre screw of the auger
drops right into the hole before drilling. Another method is to use a
high-speed wood drill with an electric drill or a pillar drill. It does not
matter if the hole is not perfect as it can be shaped with a round file.
Empty out the chippings from the chamber and any loose membrane.
Blow across the hole to discover the note of the cavity. The method
of blowing is the same as blowing across the top of a bottle to make
it sound. The pitch of the resonator is the note to which the bar has
to be tuned.

To hear the note of the bar, support it roughly a quarter of the
way in from each end on the underside, and tap the centre with a
beater. The deeper the note, the softer the beater must be (see sec-

37

tion on beaters). To raise the note, shorten the bar, but do not cut too much off at a time. To lower the note, lengthways strips can be sliced off the bar to make it more flexible. For small adjustments the note can be lowered by filing mid-way on the underside with a half-round file. The note can be raised fractionally by filing the ends of the bar.

The note of the bar should be tested against the resonator note. Get someone to help you by resting the bar on two fingers about a quarter of the way in from each end. Strike the bar in the centre and bring the resonator hole directly under the striking point. Decide whether the two sounds are in close sympathy or conflicting, and tune accordingly.

The next stage is to find the nodal points on the bar (figure 17). Some fine sawdust is needed, and two narrow strips of foam sponge to support the bar. Position the strips of sponge so that the bar rests on them about a quarter of the way in at each end, and sprinkle saw-dust on the bar. Gently tap the bar at its centre, and the sawdust will begin to fall off. Continue until there are two places where the dust accumulates. Move the supports so that they are directly underneath the dust piles. This will help the bar to vibrate correctly, and so define the nodal points more clearly. You may find the bar vibration

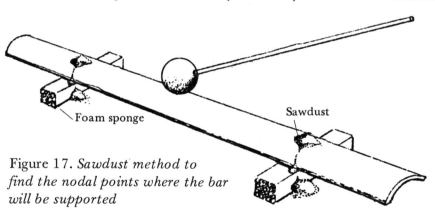

Figure 17. *Sawdust method to find the nodal points where the bar will be supported*

is not quite true and the dust piles are not in the centre of the curve. The points can be centralised by altering the angle at which you tap the bar. Sometimes the dust will not take up a definite strong position, in which case, mark a point in the centre of the curve. The two points can now be drilled with a $\frac{7}{32}$ inch twist drill. Place the bar on the resonator, directly over the hole. Mark through the nodal holes in the bar, through to the resonator. Make sure that the marks are dead centre of the bar holes.

The nails which are to be set into the resonator to support the bar are $\frac{3}{32}$ inch thick. The holes to be drilled into the resonator should be $\frac{5}{64}$ inch, so that the nail will be a tight fit (figure 18). Slide a 2 cm

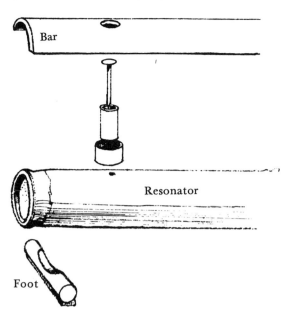

Bar

Resonator

Foot

Figure 18

length of plastic fuel pipe onto each nail head so that the plastic butts against the nail head. Now slide 1 cm of rubber tube over the plastic, leaving the nail head and 1 cm of plastic tube showing. Fit the nail supports into the bamboo resonator. If it seems that the nail may split the bamboo, enlarge the hole slightly with a round needle file. The bar will now sit above the resonator. If there is still a small discrepancy in the tuning of the bar to the resonator, further filing can be done.

Lastly, make the foot. Cut 5 cm of $\frac{1}{2}$ inch diameter dowel, and shape it to fit the curve of the bamboo where it is to be glued. To do this, hold a piece of fine sandpaper firmly round the bamboo where the foot is to be glued. Sand the dowel on the paper so that it takes the curve of the bamboo. Now sand off the surface of the bamboo at the glue point, as glue will not adhere to the shiny surface. Glue the foot into position with wood/wood glue. Make sure the instrument is stable. When the glue is dry, stick on the sponge draught excluder. Although a second foot is not necessary, you may wish to fit one.

Beaters

The type of beater used, can make all the difference to the sound from a percussion instrument. These four designs range from soft to hard, and are suitable for the percussion instruments in the book.

SOFT BEATER

Description   Length 21 cm, head width 3 cm.

Pitch   Indistinct.

Playing   Holding loosely near the end, allow for the repercussion from the combined reaction of the head bounce and the instrument vibration.

Acoustics   Largely damaged by the softness.

Making   Cut off 1.5 cm of $\frac{3}{4}$ inch diameter aluminium tubing. File clean. Cut off enough $\frac{1}{2}$ inch sponge draught excluder with a sticky back, to go round the cut tube twice. Stick one more round of sponge tube around the middle. Using $\frac{1}{2}$ inch cotton tape (the colour will not affect the sound) literally stitch, using the tape as thread, round through the hole, covering the outside edges evenly (figure 19). Overlap each width of tape, making sure the hole remains open as long as possible. Some kind of needle or spike, to help the tape through the hole, will become necessary. Finally, no more tape will go through. That is alright!

The stem, $\frac{1}{4}$ inch dowel, will jam in tightly. To ensure that the head does not fly off in a hectic passage, a small pin can be positioned

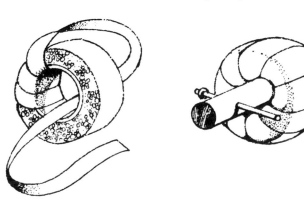

Figure 19   Figure 20

40

through the top end of the stick, against which the head must rest (figure 20). Drill a fine hole $\frac{1}{64}$ inch less than the diameter of the pin to ease the pin through the wood, and leave a small protuberance either side of the wood.

CORK BEATER

Description Length 21 cm. The cork head is the handle of a conductor's baton. The stem is cane, thickness no. 12. The cork end can be bought at a music shop and the cane from a handicraft shop. Get a piece of cane that fits tightly into the cork head.

WOODEN BEATER

Description Length 21 cm. The head is a 2 cm diameter wooden ball. The stem is cane, thickness no. 12. The wooden ball and cane can be bought in a handicraft shop.

PSEUDO RUBBER BEATER

Description Length 24 cm. A 2 cm diameter wooden ball is fitted with a rubber ring bought at a beer and winemaking shop (normally used for sealing beer bottles). The stem is cane, thickness no. 12.

41

Two-flute

This instrument began as a single flute (figure 21). The next stage was the two-flute. As far as I am aware, the design is original.

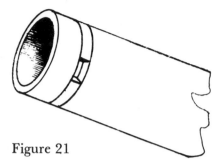

Figure 21

Description Large: length 49 cm, diameter 4.2 cm. Small: length 39 cm, diameter 3 cm. The two-flute consists of a bamboo tube designed to produce two simultaneously sounding notes. The mouthpieces are two fine slots, and opposite to these there is an opening which serves for both whistles. The lengths of tube above and below the whistles fix the pitch of each note.

Pitch Large: C, 523.3 hertz and A, 440 hertz. Small: F, 698.4 hertz and E, 659.2 hertz.

Playing Hold the instrument horizontally, and blow through the two fine slots, with the bamboo firmly against your lips. The notes can be altered by partially covering the ends of the tubes with your hands, and also by overblowing.

Acoustics The whistle system works on the same principle as a recorder, with an air duct and an edge across which the air beats. The difference is in the angle of the whistle. In the example shown, the whistle is almost at right angles to the tube, whereas in the recorder the whistle system is in line with the wooden tube. The length of the tube determines the pitch, the diameter of the tube modifies the tone.

Making Choose a length of bamboo. The piece can be cut from between two nodes, or be longer, incorporating the node, and with two open ends. The insertion of the whistles will create a tube of bamboo at either side of a centre-piece. If you are not happy with the combination of notes on completion, the tubes can be shortened to make pitch changes. If you are making a long two-flute which contains a node,

42

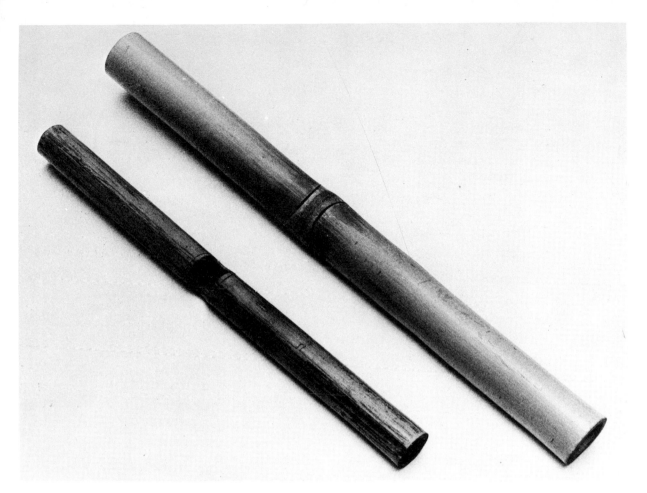

this blockage must be broken through. Either break through with a hammer and dowel, filing afterwards with a round surform, or let the whistles come either side of the node, in which case, it will be easy to file it out when you cut the bamboo.

There are two straight cuts to be made through the bamboo, and these are angled as shown in figure 22.

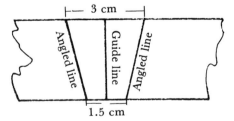

Figure 22

To help you to mark these lines, first draw a guide line that circumscribes the bamboo. Then mark two points 0.75 cm on each side

43

of the guide line; on the opposite side of the bamboo, mark two more points 1.5 cm on each side of the guide line. Join up the points to make two angled lines around the bamboo tube. (Transparent sticky tape stuck between the points will give an accurate line.)

Between the broadest parts of the two angled lines an opening must be made for the two whistles. This can be made either *before* or *after* the bamboo has been cut. In the example shown, the opening is filed out with a half-inch round file *before* the bamboo is cut. The filed opening should not penetrate more than half the width of the bamboo or be wider than 2.5 cm. (Instructions for making the hole *after* the bamboo is cut are given at the end of this section.) Using an eclipse hack-saw, or an equivalent fine blade, cut cleanly through the bamboo, following the angled lines exactly. You should now have two longish tubes and a centre-piece (figure 23).

Figure 23. *Whistle opening made* before *cutting the bamboo*

The three pieces of bamboo are now prepared for the whistles. The four surfaces produced by the two through-cuts must now be sanded perfectly flat. Put fine sandpaper on a flat surface and rub the pieces of bamboo on it with a circular motion. When the surfaces are right, you should be able to stand them on a flat surface and have good contact all round the edge. Now draw the shape of the two surfaces of the centre piece on some 0.8 mm plywood. Cut outside the shape with a pair of sharp scissors making two oversized discs. This allows for adjustment when tuning the whistle. On the centre-piece the blowing holes occur at the narrowest part. These positions must be marked on the discs for the whistle gaps. Draw the whistle gaps on the discs and cut out the pieces not required (see figure 24 for proportions). These discs will be sandwiched between the three bamboo pieces.

Figure 24. *Proportion your mouthpiece from this drawing*

Test the whistles before gluing all the parts together. Hold two bamboo pieces together (centre and one side), with the respective plywood disc in-between, and blow through the channel created by the missing piece of plywood. Use this procedure for both whistles. If the note is not clear, move the disc backwards and forwards slightly until it gives the best sound. Re-cut the whistle gap if necessary.

Now hold all the parts together so that the two blow holes are in line with each other, and the minimum distance apart (figure 25). Blow through both slits together, listening for both notes to sound.

44

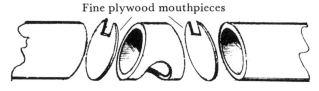

Fine plywood mouthpieces

Figure 25

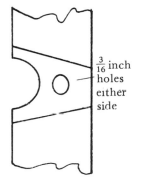

$\frac{3}{16}$ inch holes either side

Figure 26. *Drill in the same way for both kinds of opening*

Figure 27. *Whistle opening made after cutting the bamboo*

If only one note sounds, the whistle opening is not large enough, causing the two whistles to combine acoustically and one note to dominate. This fault can be cured when all the parts have been glued together. Using wood/wood glue, glue the discs onto the bamboo centre-piece first. Allow to set for fifteen minutes, and then glue this to one of the longer sections, and hold gently in a vice. Allow another fifteen minutes for the glue to set. The top half can be glued on and the instrument left upright in the vice, to dry completely. After this, any protruding plywood can be filed off, and the instrument can be tested for sound. If the two notes are not distinct two small holes, $\frac{3}{16}$ inch, can be drilled in the centre-piece, as in figure 26. This renders the centre-piece acoustically inactive.

The final adjustment is to the pitch. This is done by cutting down the tubes. If you have access to an electric sanding belt, use it to alter the tube lengths by small amounts. If you are using a saw, be cautious.

Now here is a second method of making an opening. A complete section of bamboo is cut from the bamboo centre-piece after the bamboo has been sawn into three parts (figure 27). The section to be removed is taken from the broadest point in the centre-piece, measured on the cross-section. The bamboo to be removed is one third of the total circumference. It can be split out with a knife or chisel or cut out with a fine hack-saw. If this second method is used, the discs for the mouthpieces must be made before altering the centre-piece.

Double bird whistle

The bird whistle is made commercially in the form of a small tin (figure 28) whirled around on the end of a string. Bamboo seemed to be the material for an instrument of two or more notes.

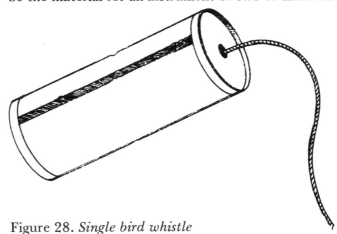

Figure 28. *Single bird whistle*

Description Length 28 cm, exterior diameter 2.5 cm. The whistle has three nodes, the middle one centrally positioned. It is connected to a handle by a piece of nylon line. Length of whistle slots 10.5 and 8 cm, width 7 mm. The whistle slots are set 90° apart round the circumference of the bamboo (figure 29).

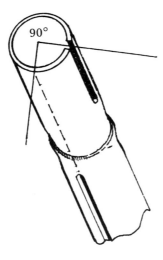

Figure 29. *Cross-sections through bamboo showing the relationship between the two whistle slots*

Pitch A♯, 466.2 hertz; G, 392 hertz.

Playing Use the instrument either inside, if there is space, or outside. Holding the handle, whirl the whistle round your head.

Acoustics When the wind crosses at 90° to the slot, the whistle sounds. Due to the nylon line twisting, the bamboo sometimes spins, causing each whistle to sound separately. The two bamboo chambers are of nearly the same capacity. To produce two pitches, each slot must be a different length. The longer the slot, the smaller the effective size of the cavity. The smaller the cavity, the higher the note, and vice versa.

Making Cut and clean up the bamboo. Mark the slot positions and lengths. Drill holes at either end of these using a $\frac{1}{4}$ inch twist drill. Now, using a pad-saw make a straight cut between the holes. The excess bamboo can be cut away with a knife. Make sure that the knife does not cut beyond the drill holes. Finish the slots with a file. Drill a $\frac{1}{16}$ inch hole in one end of the bamboo. Thread a length of nylon thread through the hole and then knot the end. A short piece of bamboo or dowel will suffice as a handle. Drill a hole half-way along the dowel, thread the nylon through and knot it securely.

47

Conch shell

This shell quite often ends up as an ornament. After the operation it can still look good on the mantlepiece, but it will then also be a trumpet.

Description   This instrument is really a horn with a simple mouthpiece shaped in the top end of the spiral structure of the shell. The spiral is approximately 110 cm long. The sound comes out of the large opening.

Pitch   Approximately D, 293.7 hertz (fundamental).

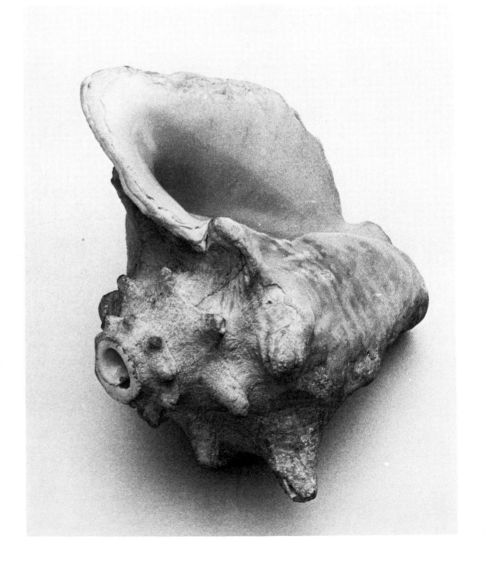

Playing   Press your lips together into the mouthpiece, as with any of the brass family, and blow hard. This may take some practice but as soon as your lips start buzzing, the instrument will sound.

Acoustics   The lips act like reeds vibrating together. The shell has a natural spiral ending in a flare. This is the ideal shape for a horn. The spiral tube in the shell has a natural harmonic range. When your lips beat at approximately 293 hertz, the fundamental note of the shell sounds.

   Being a primitive mouthpiece, the harmonic range only covers the fundamental and first harmonic. The second note is an octave above the first and requires tighter lipping and more air pressure.

Making   Conch shells may be found at seaside resorts in gift or curiosity shops. The only modification to the shell is the making of the mouthpiece. The point of the spiral must be cut off to reveal the inside of the spiral. The hole is approximately 2 cm across from the outside edges. It is best to grind the end down (use a carborundum disc, an electric sander, or a coarse file), and keep testing the hole for ease of blowing. Finish off with fine wet and dry sandpaper.

Coconut ocarina

This type of instrument is a globular flute. The Chinese version is called a 'hsuan' (figure 30) and in Europe, a more recent model, the ocarina (figure 31) was invented by an Italian. With a little carpentry I have converted the coconut into an ocarina.

Figure 30. *Chinese 'hsuan'*

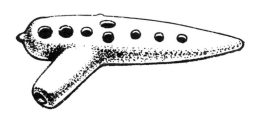

Figure 31. *Ocarina*

Description	Coconut: 12 cm by 9 cm. Bamboo mouthpiece: length 7 cm, diameter 1.5 cm.
Pitch	B, 246.9 hertz to B, 493.9 hertz. Major scale, using seven finger holes.
Playing	Blow gently through the tube. Put all fingers down for the lowest note. The scale ascends from the smallest hole: lift the fingers in sequence. The top note is the top hole of the three grouped together.
Acoustics	The sound, particularly the bottom note, is nearly pure, with no harmonic overtones. Unlike the flute, the position of the finger holes on the coconut is not important other than for convenience of playing. The size of the holes is important. The instrument will not over-

blow (that is, it will not rise an octave, creating another major scale) but by blowing very hard a high-pitched whistle can be made.

Making Choose a coconut: the larger the specimen the deeper the scale. Remove the hair and fibres and sand down the nut surface. The coconut has three eyes at one end. One is particularly soft and can be pierced with a $\frac{1}{4}$ inch twist drill. The milk can now be drained out, and the nut sliced in half. Using a tenon-saw, cut through the middle. If there is no one to help you to steady the nut, put it in a vice, remembering that, being a hard wood, the nut will crack if too much pressure is exerted. Make the cut as clean as possible, as the two halves have to be joined together again.

Remove the white kernel. (You may eat it.) Now glue the halves together again, with wood/wood glue, and secure temporarily with sticky tape. The final sanding of the surface can be done when the glue is dry.

Now the hole used to drain out the milk is shaped to become the wind hole. First, file it into a square, 11 mm by 11 mm, with a flat needle file. One of the edges must be filed to form the edge across

51

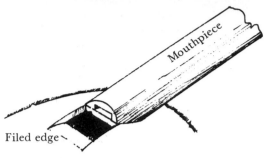

Figure 32

which the air will pass (figure 32). The bamboo tube has to be set on the opposite edge so that the air stream will strike the filed edge. The bamboo must be shaped (with a file) so that there is only a small opening when the tube is set on the edge of the hole (figure 33).

Figure 33. *Cross-section of a whistle*

The angle of the bamboo tube is critical for good tone. This can only be found by filing and test blowing until the strongest sound is produced. The pipe must then be glued with wood/wood glue in that position and held there with sticky tape until thoroughly dry.

The instrument is now ready for the finger holes (figure 34). Hold

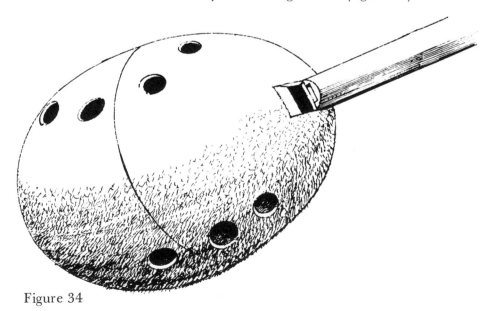

Figure 34

the instrument as if you are playing it, and mark where your fingers feel best placed. The holes will be drilled directly under where your finger pads are. Deal with each hole in sequence, starting with your little finger. Drill a $\frac{1}{16}$ inch hole and listen to the change of pitch. If you want a major scale, the note above the bottom note must rise one tone. Enlarge the hole with successive drill bits until the required note is achieved. The opening of the hole can be slightly broadened on the surface, for ease of playing, by lightly drilling with a counter-sinker. Move on to the next finger position and drill a hole smaller than the previous finished hole and enlarge it to the required note. The finger holes will get larger and you may not have large enough drill bits. In this case, use a round file to enlarge the holes. You can include a thumb hole too if you wish to go higher than an octave. Do not let the upper hole get too near the whistle hole as the sound can become a little breathy.

Coconut drums

Before making this instrument I had already been making drums with clay bodies and wooden tops (figure 35). Gluing wood to clay never proved satisfactory, so I experimented with coconuts. These have two advantages in that they are strong and easy to glue.

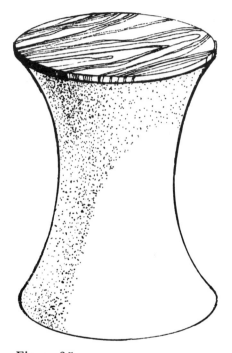

Figure 35

Description — Length 23 cm, width 14 cm. Head diameters 11 and 9 cm approximately. Two coconuts are emptied of their contents and the outsides are sanded. Each nut is fitted with a wooden head and then they are glued together.

Pitch — A, 440 hertz and D, 587.4 hertz approximately.

Playing — The drums are held between the knees (felt stuck on the coconuts helps to stop the drums slipping on clothing). The heads can either be beaten with very soft beaters or played with the hands. For hand-playing, the middle fingers may prove best. They must be relaxed and allowed on impact with the head to make contact from the ends of the fingers to the middle points between the first and second joints.

The fingers must be left in contact with the head so that all the force of the blow is absorbed, producing maximum sound. Keep the wrists below the level of the heads, and the action light. Heavy rigid playing will bring blisters very rapidly. The key factor is keeping the hands relaxed.

Acoustics   The pitch of each drum is dictated by the size of the head. The coconut chamber modifies the sound. This modification can be varied according to how the coconut is treated. If the chamber is sealed when the wooden head is fitted, the sound will be bright and the resonance of the chamber will not be very audible. If the chamber has an opening, its resonance will combine with the bright tone of the head. In the example shown, where the two coconuts join there is a hole connecting the two chambers. The striking of either or both heads activates both chambers together. The heads are of 3-ply, hence the wood grain runs in two directions. This helps the vibrations to spread across the heads. The heads must not be under stress, that is, they must be perfectly flat. This enables them to vibrate to their maximum capacity.

Making   There are three eyes on a coconut, one is particularly soft, and can be easily penetrated with a $\frac{1}{4}$ inch twist drill to drain out the milk.

The next stage is to divide the coconut cleanly with a tenon-saw. A round head will vibrate more reliably than an oval one, so it is important to cut the nut making a round section. Usually I expect to discard that part of the nut with three eyes, but it is possible to make two drums from one large coconut.

When cutting the coconut, the diameter of the cross-section can be varied from the maximum diameter down to 9 cm. A smaller head than this is difficult to sound without heavy playing. Next, remove the flesh from the nut or nuts. Now you have sustenance! The rim produced by the cut must be perfectly true so that when the edge is placed on a smooth surface, there is good contact all the way round. This is where a good saw cut can reduce the correction work on the rim. If machine sanders are not available, smoothing the rim is best done with medium sandpaper, putting a full sheet on a flat surface, holding the coconut firmly, and revolving it on the sandpaper. Finish with fine sandpaper.

Use 1.5 mm plywood for the heads. Place the rim on the plywood sheet and draw round the edge. A good pair of sharp scissors will cut the ply, keeping 2 mm outside the line. Run wood/wood glue all along the rim and fit the head on. If the plywood has a good smooth side let this be on top. Using sticky tape, stick four strips across the heads and down the sides. Make sure that glue is squashed out along the whole edge of the rim. Where this does not happen, use more tape. Six hours in a warm dry atmosphere is enough to set the glue for further work. Remove the tape, and with a medium-fine hand-file, take off the excess plywood that protrudes over the coconut edge. File downwards towards the coconut sides or around the plywood edge. It is important that this edge is smooth and rounded to the touch, as any burrs or sharp edges will aggravate your fingers when playing. Sand off the hair of the nut with a coarse paper,

Figure 36. *Coconut drum components*

finishing this and the head with flour or garnet paper. When sanding plywood, follow the grain.

You now have a single unattached drum. If you wish to have the cavity open, saw off the bottom end of the coconut, and clean up with a round file. Repeat these instructions for the second drum. I find the joining of two drums the most difficult part. The perfect rims that were made for the heads have now to be produced in miniature on one side of each drum for an exact fit (figure 36). It is preferable to have the two heads as much on the same plane as possible. Cut off a disc with a fine saw, producing a hole and a small rim on each nut. Sand both until they are approximately equal in diameter, and fit snugly together. Now they can be glued and, if possible, taped together whilst setting.

Finally, stick a patch of felt on the far side of each drum.

Tin-can maraca

I am interested in converting throwaway objects into instruments. The tin cans shown fit together very well to form a shape well suited for maracas.

The body may also be made of clay, plastic, wood or metal, with beads of lead shot inside.

Description   Large: length 14 cm, width 11 cm. Small: length 12 cm, width 8.5 cm. Two tin cans are soldered together at the rim, to make one maraca. Each contains fine lead-shot fishing weights.

Playing   To create definite rhythms the contents must be thrown in a packed form back and forth in the maraca. To do this the maraca is best held with both hands, and the movement of the hands and arms must be rhythmically precise, encouraging a crisp sound.

Acoustics   The pitch in each case is indefinite, but the larger tin cavity gives the

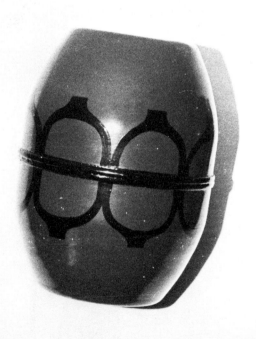

deeper sound. The quality of sound can be modified by holding the maraca different ways when shaking.

Making Remove all grease from the rims of the tins to be soldered together. Using a 60 W soldering iron, tin both rims well. The amount of lead shot used is a personal choice. I used about two small packets in the large maraca and one packet in the small maraca. Put the shot in one half. Place the other half on top so that the rims come together (figure 37). Now run the hot iron along the two edges until they melt and join. Do this all the way round, and if finally there are some holes, fill these in with more solder. Fine wet and dry sandpaper will finish the job ready for painting if you so wish.

Figure 37. *Tin-can maraca components*

59

Coconut maraca

Like the tin-can shape, the coconut shape is suitable as a maraca. It is just a matter of taking a look under all that hair.

Description One coconut containing fine lead shot.

Pitch Indefinite.

Playing As described for the tin-can maraca.

Acoustics As the coconut is fibrous wood, its resonance is less harsh than a tin can.

Making Drill out the soft eye of the coconut with a $\frac{1}{4}$ inch twist drill. Drain off the milk. Cut the nut in half with a tenon-saw, making sure of a clean cut. Remove the contents. Redrill the drainage hole with a $\frac{1}{2}$ inch twist drill so it can be plugged with $\frac{1}{2}$ inch dowel. Glue the two halves of the nut together with wood/wood glue and clamp until dry. Pour two packets of lead shot through the hole into the nut. Plug and glue the hole with $\frac{1}{2}$ inch dowel. Leave to dry. Cut off excess dowel and clean up the outside of the coconut with sandpaper.

Tin fiddle

I designed this instrument specifically to make use of a junk object — the tin can. A friend lent me a fiddle acquired in Hong Kong, which I have identified as a 'gihyan' (figure 38). The neck passes through the coconut body, and this simplifies structural problems. I also decided to use a fret-board, as a fiddle I had made previously, based on the Javanese 'rebab' (figure 39) had proved more than difficult to play.

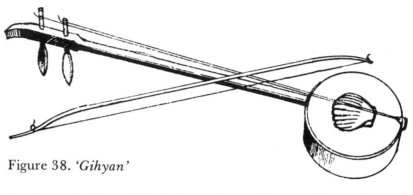

Figure 38. *'Gihyan'*

Description Total length 58 cm. Tin: height 10 cm, diameter 10 cm (approximately). Fretboard: length 38 cm, cross-section 1 inch × $\frac{1}{4}$ inch. Dowel: length 58 cm, diameter $\frac{5}{8}$ inch. Wire guide: height $\frac{1}{4}$ inch; cross-section 1 inch × $\frac{1}{4}$ inch. (Hardwood cross-section 1 inch × $\frac{1}{4}$ inch, is available from 'do-it-yourself' shops.)

The wire used is either 4 or 5 gauge piano wire or a guitar E string. A violin peg and a cockle shell will also be needed. The adjustable frets, which are optional, are made from 18 lb breaking strain nylon line.

Pitch A, 440 hertz.

Playing In a sitting position, gently grip the can between your knees. The peg can rest against your chest. Your hand is now free to move up and down the finger-board whilst bowing with the other hand. Bow between the shell bridge and the end of the fret-board.

Acoustics The sound box is a tin which is open at the bottom. The top of the tin is the belly of the instrument. The cavity amplifies lateral vibrations coming from the wire through the shell and top. Although it is a fairly rigid membrane, the top moves enough to cause the air in the tin to respond. The loudest notes occur when the wire pitch corresponds to that of the cavity. This is another instance of sym-

Figure 39.
Javanese 'rebab'

pathetic vibrations as demonstrated in the boncas, slit drum, bamboo chime bar, etc.

Making   Refer to figure 40. Two holes, the same diameter as the dowel must

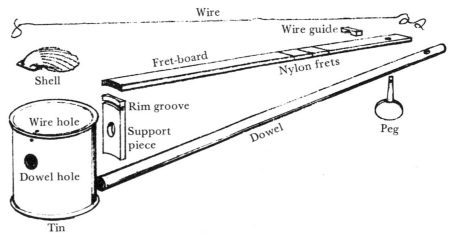

Figure 40. *Tin fiddle components*

be made in the tin. They must be exactly opposite each other and 2.5 cm down from the closed end. Use a twist drill or wood auger. If you use an auger, shape a piece of 2 inches × 1 inch softwood to fit the inside curve of the tin, into which the bit can cut. The piece of wood should be about 30 cm long, and set in a vice or clamped to the table, with the tin on one end (figure 41). The centre twist on

Drill through tin into the wood

Support wood in a vice

Figure 41

the bit pulls it down, through the tin, and into the wood on the other side. The cutter then slices out a disc of metal, without denting the tin. Repeat this procedure for the second hole.

Fit the dowel. Cut the support piece and drill a hole $\frac{5}{8}$ inch diameter with the auger, in the centre of it. To make this piece fit well, one side of it must be filed and sanded to fit the curve of the tin. Next, cut a groove in the support piece with an eclipse hack-saw to house the rim of the tin. The support piece should project above the tin rim. This is a good time to glue the parts made so far, using wood/metal glue. In the places where the tin, the dowel and the support piece make contact, use plenty of glue. The excess can be trimmed off with a knife when hard. If the support piece will not stay in position, use sticky tape to secure it until it is set. The glue needs 24 hours at room temperature. Rapid-drying resin glues are now available but I have not found them as reliable.

The next stage is the cutting of the fret-board. This sits on the support piece and the far end of the dowel. Before fixing the fret-board, its slope must be considered. This is done by putting all the fiddle parts loosely together.

A hole for the wire is now made in the tin with a $\frac{1}{16}$ inch twist drill. The wire is threaded through this hole and wound around itself. Enough wire is cut to stretch from the hole to where the peg will be, with some left over. The wire should be wound firmly. The use of pliers may score the wire causing it to break under tension; it is better to twist it between index finger and thumb, revolving the tin. Ensure that the wire is wound evenly around itself, producing a good ply, about 1.5 cm long. Cut off excess wire. Tape the fret-board into position and place the shell on the lid. (If a cockle shell is unobtainable, use half a walnut shell.) Run the wire over the shell so that it sits in one of the grooves. Continue taking the wire along the top of the fret-board and hold it taut at the peg end.

64

The height of the wire at the shell end of the fret-board should be no more than 3 mm. If the wire is too high at this point, the shell can be sanded down. If the fret-board is too close to the wire, it can be lowered by filing down the support piece. Alternatively, exchange the shell for a larger one, thus raising the bridge. Once you have adjusted the height of the fret-board, it can be made to fit close to the dowel at the peg end, by filing out a groove with a round or half-round file to fit the curve of the dowel. The groove can be 4 cm in length. Make sure too that the fret-board sits flush on the support piece at the other end.

Glue at both ends with wood/wood glue, and tape into position (Resin W dries in six hours).

The purpose of the wire-guide is to make the wire begin close to the fret-board. Make a fine groove with a fret-saw or a hack-saw across one edge of the wire-guide. This side is then glued down 5 cm from the end of the fret-board, with a piece of wire temporarily in the groove to keep it free of glue. The wire-guide must sit flush on the fret-board for good glue contact.

Drill the hole for the violin peg next. This is simple if you have a peg reamer, otherwise the hole (which is tapered) must be first drilled the same diameter as the narrowest end of the peg and shaped with a file until the peg fits snugly, projecting at the narrow end by about 2 cm. The narrow end projects upwards. Drill a $\frac{1}{32}$ inch hole in this end, close to the fret-board.

Push the wire through the fine groove in the wire-guide and through the hole in the peg. When winding the wire onto the peg, make sure that the short length first passing through the peg is bent upwards and succeeding coils wind over it and hold it firm. If the peg slips, coat it with rosin for a better grip. The wire may hold the shell bridge in position, but if it does not, glue the shell to the tin with wood/metal glue.

Finally, the nylon frets can be tied onto the fret-board. Nylon slips very easily, so make a noose in one end of the line, pass the other end through the noose, pull the two ends tight and tie twice. Slide the knot underneath the fret-board. As the frets are moveable, the kind of scale can be a personal choice.

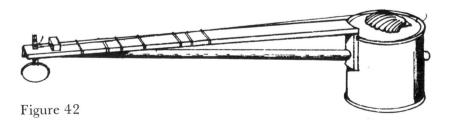

Figure 42

Fiddle bow

Initially I based my design on the bow attached to the 'gihyan' (see figure 38). The example shown below is based on a design executed by a student in a musical instrument making course which I organised.

Description   Length 70 cm. The wood is cut from a piece of pirana pine with cross-section 4 cm × 8 mm. Nylon sewing thread, a substitute for horse hair, is wound between two $\frac{1}{2}$ inch brass screws. The nylon is permanently taut.

Playing   After rubbing rosin onto the nylon, the bow will bite into the wire of your instrument. When bowing, the nylon grips the wire momentarily. The reaction of the wire is to spring back. In a simple bowing movement, the wire repeats this action many times, producing a steady note.

Making   Scale up from the drawing (figure 43) onto your piece of wood. The width of the bow is 1.4 cm (± 0.1 cm). Cut out the shape with a fret-

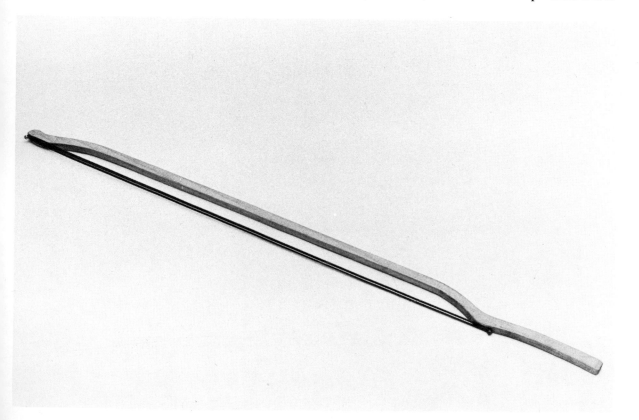

Figure 43. *Scale up to give shape*

saw or coping-saw and sand it. Rub on varnish with a cloth and wipe off all excess to seal the wood. Prick holes for the screws and drive them into the wood, leaving enough protruding for the nylon to wind round (figure 44). Tie the nylon to one end and wind round the screws. Use a complete bobbin of thread. Secure the other end. When applying rosin to the bow, the rosin block may stick to the threads. Try not to let this happen, as a thread could break, causing all the threads to come loose.

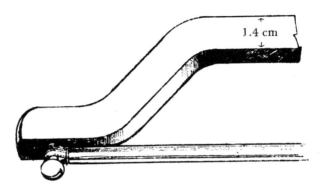

Figure 44. *Detail of winding*

Mouth bow

My instrument is modelled on that of a friend of mine from Mexico. His mouth bow was home-made and, I presume, Mexican in origin. The instrument also appears as a primitive folk instrument of the Old World.

Description Wire length approximately 1 metre no. 6 piano wire. Piece of ash length 120 cm, diameter approximately 1.5 cm. The wire passes through a $\frac{1}{16}$ inch hole at one end and is secured through a small wooden bead $\frac{3}{8}$ inch diameter. The wire can be tensioned at the other end with a violin peg. There is a smooth area, approximately 5 cm long, carved above the wooden bead, on the outer curve of the bow.

Pitch G♯, 207.6 hertz.

Playing Sit on a chair, and place the bow between your legs. The peg end rests on the ground, against your foot, the flat surface of the other end against your cheek, with your mouth slightly open. The bow is

held firmly, using the other hand to pluck the wire with a plectrum. Change the shape of the mouth to bring out different notes.

Acoustics   The wire has a fundamental note, and a series of harmonics rising above, which give the wire sound and a tone quality. Shaping the mouth cavity to an air space related in pitch to one of the harmonics, encourages that harmonic to sound as a distinct note.

Making   Use a branch which will bend, keeping the wire well tensioned. Stripping off the bark does not affect the sound.

Drill a $\frac{1}{16}$ inch hole 5 cm in from one end. Thread the wire through this hole and then through the bead, winding some wire back on itself to secure the bead. The flat area can now be shaped with a penknife.

Next the other end: if you happen to possess a peg reamer, drill a hole the size of the narrow end of the reamer, and ream out a hole. Otherwise drill a hole the size of the narrow end of the peg, and, with a small round file, make a tapering conical hole to fit the peg. Fit the peg. If it slips, coat it with rosin. If the hole in the peg is not visible, drill a fresh one, with a $\frac{1}{16}$ inch twist drill. When fitting the wire onto the peg, make sure that a short length first passed through the hole, is overwound with wire when tensioning. Have the wire tight enough for easy plucking.

69

Whirling friction drum

The name alone is fascinating, although until I saw one in action, descriptions seemed hardly believable. A student demonstrated a home-made model during one of my courses, and I was then able to work out a simple design.

I have since read that the instrument is known as 'hoo'r', in Coventry.

Description   Tin can: length 11.5 cm, diameter 7.5 cm. Card disc: diameter just less than 7.5 cm to fit in the can. Nylon cord: length approximately 1 m, knotted at both ends. Wooden handle: length 30 cm of 1 inch diameter dowel. 4 mm ply disc, diameter 6.5 cm.

Pitch   Indefinite.

Playing   Holding the wooden dowel, whirl the can round on the cord.

Acoustics   Rosin is rubbed into the wooden dowel at the base of the ply disc. Friction occurs between the cord and the rosined wood. The vibrations pass down the taut nylon cord to the card membrane and the sound is modified by the resonance of the can chamber.

Making   The can is an average food tin (figure 45). Remove both ends. With

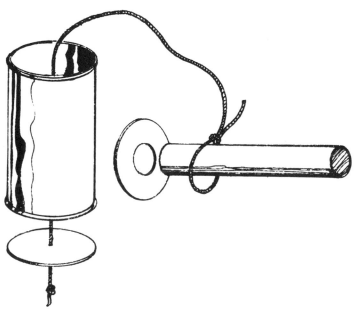

Figure 45. *Whirling friction drum components*

70

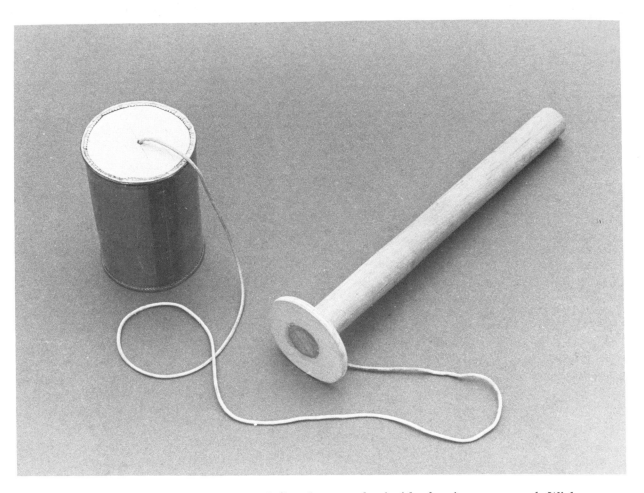

pliers, squash flat the cut edge inside the tin, at one end. With a
screwdriver, prise out the cut edge at the other end. The card disc
will butt against this metal edge. Cut a card disc the same diameter as
the inside of the can, using a pair of compasses to draw the circle,
and pierce through the centre. Fit the card in the can so that it jams
against the metal edge. Knot the cord and thread it through the hole
in the card.

Now make the handle. Using a pair of compasses draw two circles
on the 4 mm plywood. The larger one is 6.5 cm in diameter, and the
smaller, drawn inside it, is 2.5 cm. The smaller circle can now be
drilled out, to take the dowel. Use a brace and bit, and when the
auger bit has just penetrated through the ply, finish drilling from the
other side, in order to make a clean hole. The ply disc can be cut with
a coping-saw and sanded afterwards. Fit the disc to the dowel, and
glue with wood/wood glue. When the glue is dry, the cord can be
knotted in a single loop round the dowel. Make sure the base of the
ply disc is smooth where the rosin is to be rubbed on. Now you can
give it a whirl.

71

Ceramic flute

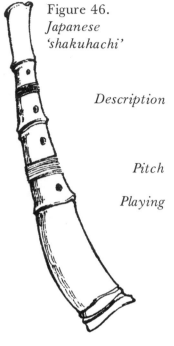

Figure 46.
*Japanese
'shakuhachi'*

A process not unlike casting with molten metal is to cast with liquid clay (called slip). I decided to make a flute in ceramic, based on the Japanese 'shakuhachi' (figure 46). Because of the mould, my instrument has an entirely different appearance.

Description Length 44 cm, diameter 19 cm, wall thickness 1.5 mm. This is a notch flute. The notch serves as a mouthpiece and the ceramic tube is completely hollow with six finger holes.

Pitch F♯, 370 hertz, rising two octaves.

Playing Place the top of the instrument under your lower lip, with the notch facing outwards. Direct a fine air stream across the top edge of the notch. The fingering is straightforward. All fingers are put down for the bottom note and raised in succession for the scale. The octave is achieved with all fingers down and overblowing, this register being played with the same fingering as the first. The top F requires overblowing into the next register again, using the two holes below the top one.

Acoustics The flute sound is produced by air vibrating across the lip (figure 47). The air stream passes outside, causing a change of pressure inside the flute chamber. The air is then drawn inside the lip to compensate. The pressure rises inside the flute chamber, thus redirecting the air stream outwards again. This action causes the air to beat and sets the column of air in the tube in motion. With all finger holes covered, the column of air is the same length as the tube. When the bottom hole is opened, the sounding length is shortened and so on.

The size of each hole, in relation to its position, is important. If the bottom hole were placed further up the tube, it would need to be smaller, and if placed further down the tube, it would need to be larger. At the bottom of the instrument, the optimum size of the holes should be the same as the diameter of the tube, but this would make fingering difficult without mechanical pads, so the holes are smaller and further up the tube. This means that the tone is slightly less full, but with no less character.

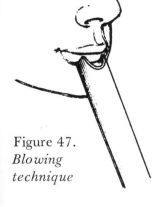

Figure 47.
*Blowing
technique*

Making Some facilities for pottery-making are necessary. The process entails slip casting and therefore making a mould. The example shown is made of porcelain, but earthenware or stoneware are also satisfactory.

First make a plaster mould to cast your clay tube in. The former,

72

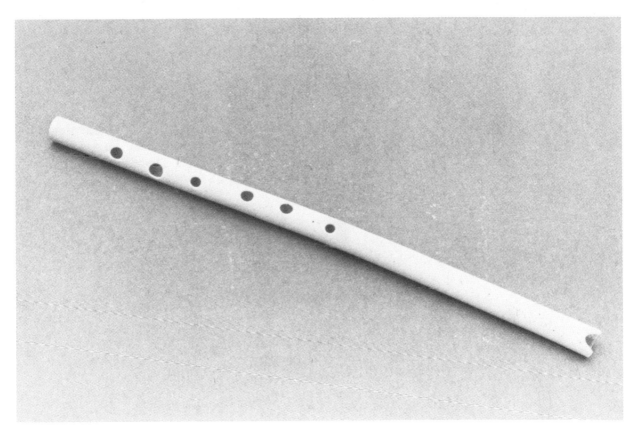

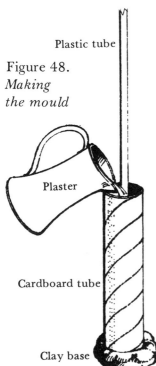

Plastic tube

Figure 48.
*Making
the mould*

Plaster

Cardboard tube

Clay base

which is the male shape and the model for the flute, is 21 mm over-flow system plastic tube, bought at builder's suppliers. The plaster mould can be made in a cardboard tube, the kind that carpets are rolled round, approximately 10 cm in diameter. Cut 70 cm length of cardboard tube and a 2 m length of plastic tube. The plastic tube should be as smooth as possible, as this will create the inside surface of the mould. If there is roughness, use very fine wet and dry sandpaper (no. 600). Rub washing-up liquid all over the outside of the tube and let it dry. This helps the tube to slide out of the plaster.

Stand the cardboard tube upright, blocking the bottom end with clay (figure 48). Stand the plastic tube in the cardboard tube, setting it firmly in the centre of the clay base. Now mix up the plaster. Pour water into a plastic bowl. (Make more than you think you may need, in case there is a leak in the cardboard mould.) Start strewing plaster into the water with your hand. Continue until the surface appears solid and begins to craze. Now stir the mixture thoroughly, the right consistency is a thickish creamy mix.

Use a funnel or a large jug to pour the plaster into the mould. If the plaster seems a bit lumpy, sieve it before pouring into the tube. Be ready to patch up any plaster leaks in the clay base with some extra clay. You may need someone to help you at this stage. Make

73

sure the plastic tube is in the centre of the plaster. As the plaster starts to set, it gets warm. Keep checking to see how firm it is. If your finger leaves an impression in the plaster, it is not ready. The warmth of the plaster causes the plastic tube to expand, and become tight in the plaster casing. When the plaster is firm enough, pour cold water down the plastic tube to make it contract. (It should be blocked at the bottom by the clay stop.) As the plastic tube shrinks slightly, you must pull it out of the plaster mould. There is no easy way to do this; it requires straight force to pull the two apart. The diagram (figure 49) may help you. Once the tube starts to move, it will come out cleanly.

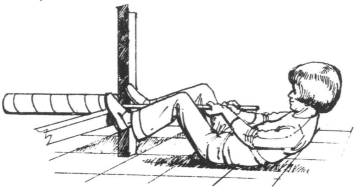

Figure 49. *Removing the plastic tube from the mould*

Next, strip off all the cardboard, leaving the plaster mould to dry out. When the mould is ready, stand it upright, and block up the bottom with clay. Mix up some clay slip and pour it in, keeping it topped up for about ten minutes. Slip that has run and dried can help you to estimate the thickness to which it has set; 2—2.5 mm is thick enough. Now drain the slip out, and pierce the bottom end to release any remaining slip. The cast must now be left to dry. This can take up to a day, depending on the condition of the mould, and the warmth of the room. As the clay tube dries, it shrinks, and will slide out of the mould. You may need to push one end gently. The clay tube should be in a leather-hard state. If it is drier, the clay will crack when it is worked.

Cut both ends of the tube with a sharp knife to give a clean edge. The first stage is to make the notched mouthpiece. Follow the diagram (figure 50) and use a sharp blade. You must master the technique of blowing at this stage, or you will not be able to proceed any further. Roughly speaking, a tube 60 cm long will sound middle C. Tune the tube by cutting down the length.

The next stage is the making of the holes, using a set of twist drills and a fine countersinker. The holes must be made in order, starting with the bottom hole, and only moving on to the next when the note of the first is what you require. As a guide, try starting the first

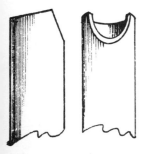

Figure 50. *Notch detail*

74

hole 6 cm from the bottom. Start the hole fairly small, and enlarge it until you reach the required note. Countersink the edge of the hole every time you use a larger drill bit, so that the edge of the hole does not get chipped. When the hole is right, it can be slightly countersunk for more comfortable fingering.

Remember that the clay tube is very fragile, and that great care must be taken when handling it. Place the fingerholes where they feel comfortable. The example shown will give some idea of the spacing, but be prepared for a little experimentation. Cast a few clay tubes to get the best results. When the flute is completed, dry it thoroughly before biscuit-firing. After it is fired, wet and dry sandpaper the surface of the flute. You may find that you can improve the mouthpiece of the flute with wet and dry sandpaper. Glazing is not advised, as it alters the size of the holes. A better way of finishing the instrument is to vitrify it (vitrification is a high-firing at 1200 °C+). This process reveals the characteristics of the clay, giving the instrument a finish and toughness. Of course, the very materials imply that it is a fragile instrument, but the sound is so good as to make it worth the extra care.

Cracker

This is an imitation of the Japanese 'bin-sasara' (figure 51), an instrument used in Shinto and folk music.

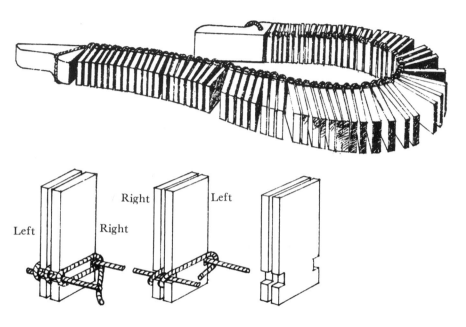

Figure 51. *Japanese 'bin-sasara'*

Description 60 hardwood squares, each 3 inches × 3 inches × $\frac{1}{4}$ inch thick, slung on a nylon cord passing through $\frac{1}{4}$ inch holes positioned 1 cm from the edge and half-way along ('Ramin' hardwood is available at 'do-it-yourself' shops). The handles are $\frac{3}{4}$ inch dowel 7 cm long, drilled through with a $\frac{1}{4}$ inch twist drill. There is 9 cm of spare cord between the slabs and the handles.

Pitch Indefinite.

Playing Hold the handles and let the slabs rest against your clenched fingers. Alternately raise and lower each end very quickly, pushing your knuckles into the rising slabs. The action sends a chain reaction of movements through the slabs, producing a cracking effect.

Acoustics The slabs act as beaters as well as sounding pieces. The sound lasts as long as the action because all the slabs are damped by each other when the movement stops.

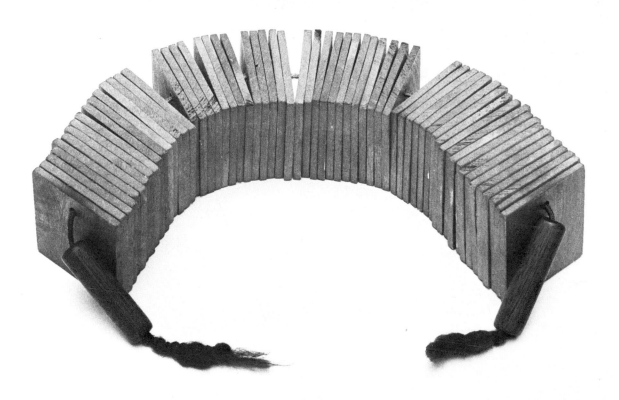

Making Cut up a length of 3 inch × $\frac{1}{4}$ inch hardwood to make about 60 pieces. Drill $\frac{1}{4}$ inch holes half-way along one side and 1 cm in from the edge in each slab. Neaten with sandpaper. Thread nylon cord (no. 1, 600 lb breaking strain) through the slabs. Cut two pieces of dowel 7 cm long and drill lengthways through the centre with a $\frac{1}{4}$ inch twist drill. Finish with sandpaper. Thread the cord through the handles and knot each end, leaving approximately 9 cm of cord extra between the handles and the end slabs, when pulled tight.

Tube drums

Initially I had been using cardboard carpet tubes for making plaster moulds (see section on ceramic flute). The coconut drums were only one of a series of wooden-headed drums which I designed and made. Apart from the coconut drums, I experimented with ceramic tube drums (figure 52). Gluing wood to cardboard proved reliable and the choice of lengths is considerable. The nearest relative is the 'boobams' (not illustrated) with metal cylindrical bodies and skin heads.

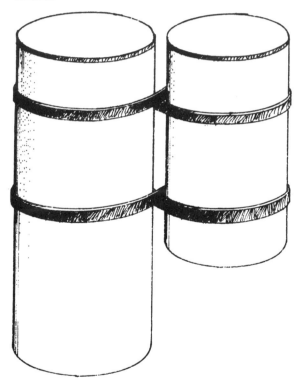

Figure 52. *Ceramic tube drums*

Description   Overall height 96 cm. There are eight cardboard tubes with tops made from 1.5 mm plywood. Three tubes, 29, 31.5 and 36 cm long, are 8.5 cm in diameter. Five tubes, 39.5, 46, 49, 55 and 62 cm long, are 9.5 cm in diameter. The drums are supported on a chromium-plated tube, length 76 cm, diameter $\frac{5}{8}$ inch. This is set into a wooden base.

Pitch   C, 130.6 hertz to C, 261.6 hertz, major scale.

78

Playing   Use either a light but firm touch with the hands, or soft beaters.

Acoustics   The plywood tops are not under tension, so the pitch is controlled by the length of the tubes.

Making   Cardboard tubing is available from carpet shops. Take a saw when collecting as the tubes are sometimes 3.5 m long. One end of each cardboard tube must be perfectly flat, so that the plywood head can vibrate freely when glued. The best way to cut the cardboard cleanly is on a band-saw.

Draw round the cardboard tubes onto your 1.5 mm plywood sheet. These are the drum heads, cut them out with scissors. Glue them onto the tops of the tubes with wood/wood glue, and secure temporarily with sticky tape. If the pitch of the drums is not to your liking, you can alter it thus: to raise the pitch, shorten the tube, and to lower the pitch, partially cover the opening with fine plywood. Arrange the tubes in a group (figure 53) and glue together with wood/wood glue. In the example shown, I have organised the drums in three tiers in order to give a leading edge for hand playing.

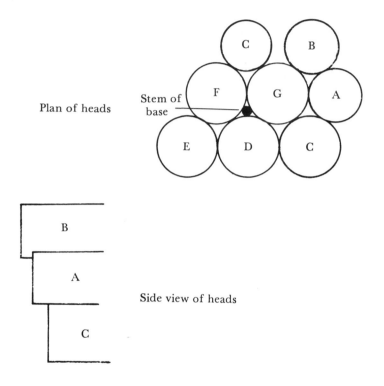

Plan of heads

Stem of base

Side view of heads

Figure 53

Cut the wood for the base (figure 54). Glue together with wood/wood glue. When set, drill out a hole ($\frac{1}{2}$ inch diameter, depth 4 cm) for the dowel piece ($\frac{1}{2}$ inch diameter, length 15 cm). Fit and glue.

Force a slightly oversized piece of dowel, 15 cm long, into the chromed tube, a distance of 5 cm. Drive the chromed tube into a centrally positioned space between the cardboard drums from the underneath, so that the wooden end is just visible at the top (figure 53). Run plenty of wood/wood glue (Resin W) down around the wooden end so that it is bonded securely to the cardboard tubes.

When all the parts are dry, the instrument can be set onto its wooden base. The chromed tube can be glued with wood/metal glue to the protruding dowel in the wooden base.

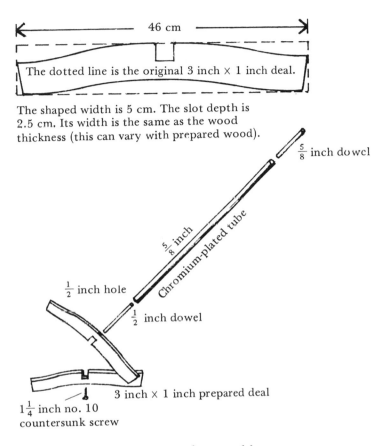

The dotted line is the original 3 inch × 1 inch deal.

46 cm

The shaped width is 5 cm. The slot depth is 2.5 cm. Its width is the same as the wood thickness (this can vary with prepared wood).

$\frac{5}{8}$ inch dowel

$\frac{5}{8}$ inch

Chromium-plated tube

$\frac{1}{2}$ inch hole

$\frac{1}{2}$ inch dowel

3 inch × 1 inch prepared deal

$1\frac{1}{4}$ inch no. 10 countersunk screw

Figure 54. *General pattern for wood base*

Ceramic chimes

This instrument is very much a prototype, with many modifications still to be attempted. I was interested in discovering the sound of fired clay bars in an instrument modelled on the xylophone (figure 55) and metalophone (figure 56). Details of casting the clay bars appear in the section on the ceramic flute, but replace the 21 mm plastic former tube with a 32 or 44 mm tube of the same plastic. When the clay tubes are cast, slice them laterally down the centre with a fine stretched wire. After biscuit-firing, the nodal points can be found in the same manner as discussed in the section on the bamboo chime.

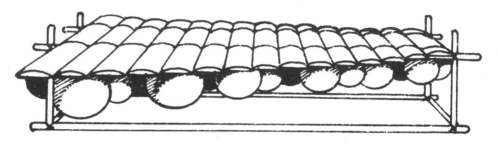

Figure 55. *African xylophone*

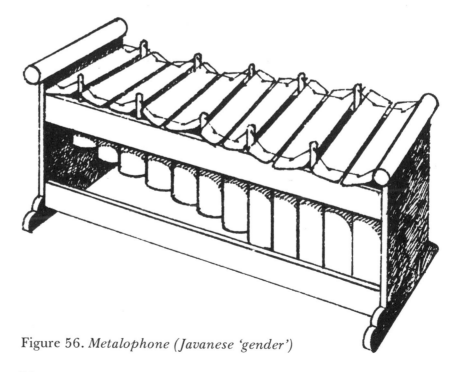

Figure 56. *Metalophone (Javanese 'gender')*

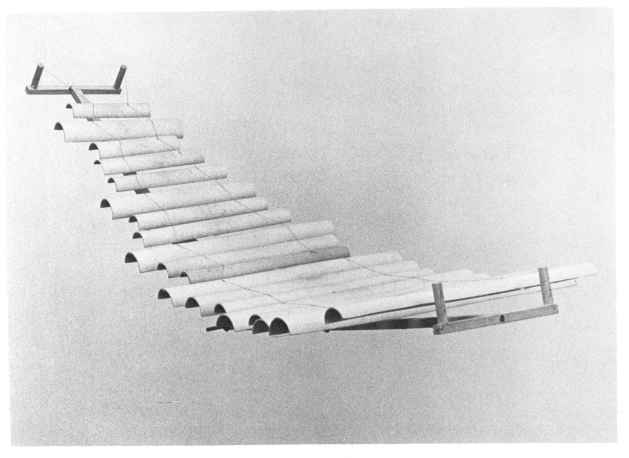

Drill the fired clay with a $\frac{1}{8}$ inch glass-cutting drill. The bars can then be high-fired to toughen them. The bars are then threaded together, as shown in figure 57.

Tuning is not easy, so the scale in the example shown is a random ascent from A, 440 hertz to B♭, 1864.8 hertz. Cork beaters produce a clear ringing tone.

The dimensions for the support are best worked out after all the bars have been threaded together. The ends of the nylon are knotted to make sizeable loops (figure 58). The support is created by two

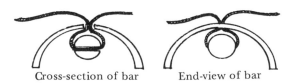

Cross-section of bar   End-view of bar

Figure 57. *Detail of threading with nylon line and wooden beads*

Knot to form nylon loop at end of the threaded bars

Figure 58

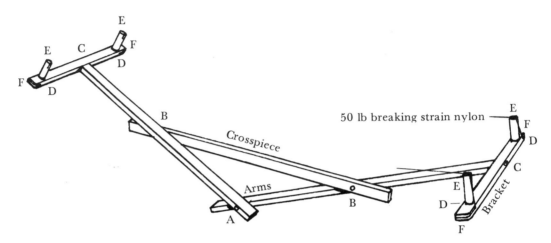

Figure 59. *Ceramic chimes support*

wooden arms (see figure 59) 1 inch × $\frac{1}{2}$ inch cross-section which are
bolted together at A. A third piece, $\frac{3}{4}$ inch × $\frac{1}{4}$ inch cross-section, is
fitted across the two arms and secured with screws at B. Two lengths
of $\frac{1}{2}$ inch square-section wood are screwed and glued to the ends C
of the wooden arms. Two pegs of $\frac{1}{2}$ inch dowel are screwed and glued
to each bracket D. The tops E of the pegs are grooved 6 mm down
with a small hack-saw, and the same cut is made to the ends F of the
brackets. Figure 60 shows how the nylon loops pass round the

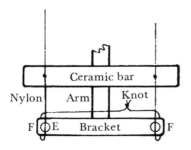

Figure 60

brackets and pegs. The angle of the arms can be adjusted by re-positioning the crosspiece, and any further slack in the nylon can be taken up by reknotting. The complete instrument can be slung from a frame or set on a stand.

Slither

The slither is a combination of ideas basic to a number of instruments. The sound-board is open underneath, with struts fanning out to the edges. The idea came from a piano, which, though a highly sophisticated instrument, has a strutted sound-board open at either side, assuming that the piano lid is raised. The bridges, which are slotted wooden balls, can be slid into any position under the wires. This idea appears in the Japanese 'koto' (figure 61) and the 'harmonic canon' of Harry Partch (not illustrated). The simple method of stringing with light wire is reminiscent of many zithers.

The slither has a separate bridge for each wire (figure 62), thus making it far more flexible. For simplicity, all the wires are the same pitch, being equal in tension, length and gauge. This means that when arranging the bridges to make a continuous tune, those bridges giving

Figure 61. *Japanese 'koto'*

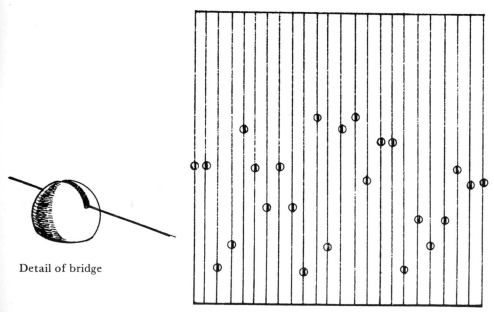

Detail of bridge

Figure 62

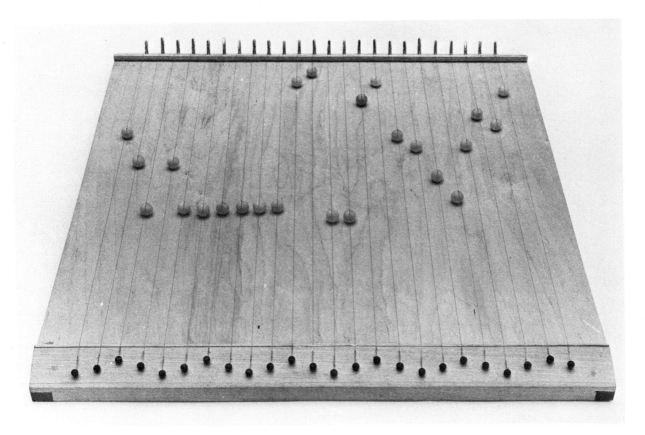

the same note will align across the sound-board. An alternative design uses a set of stretched wires, all the same length, tension and gauge. The scale would be produced by a long bridge (figure 63). With a set of seven equally-pitched wires, the bridge will produce a chromatic octave, doubling on the seventh note.

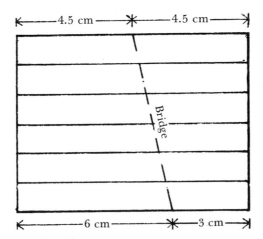

Figure 63

Fandango

I find the best way to test an idea is to draw it and then make it. Further modifications only become apparent when the components are assembled. This instrument originated from the Indian 'gopi yantra' (figure 64). Figures 65 and 66 are previous experiments based on the 'gopi yantra'. I was interested in taking the idea further, and chose a paper resonator. Although not an exact replica, it bears a resemblance to a form of cloth fan speaker used in some early gramophones.

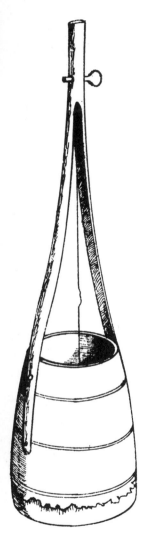

Figure 64. *Indian 'gopi yantra'*

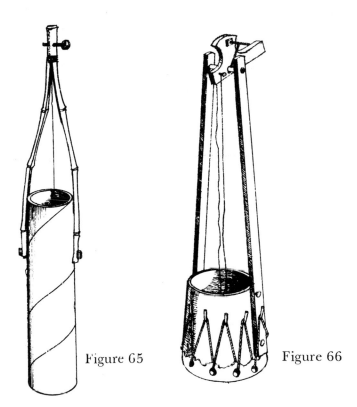

Figure 65   Figure 66

With all these instruments there is at least one wire with a tension adjuster to alter the pitch (figure 67). The wire is plucked, and the vibrations are amplified through direct contact with a stretched skin or, as in this example, by the fan. The folds in the paper make it semi-rigid ensuring that the vibrations are not absorbed. The fan, vibrating thus, increases the volume of sound of the plucked wire. The wire can also be bowed.

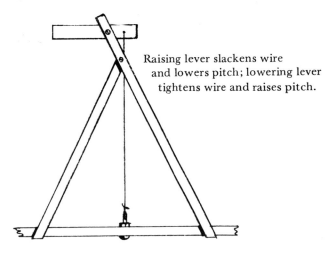

Raising lever slackens wire and lowers pitch; lowering lever tightens wire and raises pitch.

Figure 67. *Detail of lever system*

Angel bars

This is a percussion instrument using a fan resonator identical to the type used for the fandango. The initial idea came from the chiming system of a clock (figure 68). The first instrument that was developed from this is shown in figure 69. The resonator is resined canvas, and the bars are struck with soft beaters near the base. The weights on the bars are positioned to encourage the strongest harmonic in the bars to come out.

This is a fairly weighty instrument, and I was interested in developing one with thinner bars and a folding resonator (such as a paper fan). If these larger instruments are to be transportable, then they must be collapsable. For this reason I chose Dexion 'Speedframe' (square-section metal tube) for the stand. In the example shown,

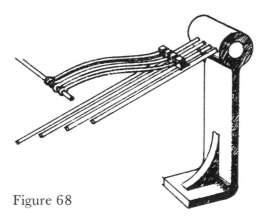

Figure 68

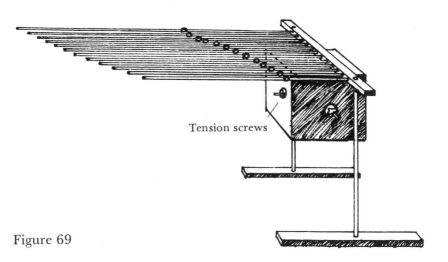

Tension screws

Figure 69

90

each bar is bent double in a U-shape, and clamped at the base. The front bar is struck with a cork beater, and its other half, which has the same pitch, rings in sympathy. The vibrations are transmitted to the fan, thus making the sounds audible.

The system is similar in principle to a tuning fork, in which one prong is struck and both prongs vibrate. The sound is made audible by pressing the stem of the tuning fork to a resonant object, the energy being passed back and forth. There have been various pianos using tuning-fork devices, one of the most recent being the Fender Rhodes electric piano.

91

Strokerphone

An idea for an experiment may come from just seeing a drawing or photograph of an instrument. In this instance, I saw a drawing of a 'nunut' (figure 70). This instrument comes from New Ireland (an island east of New Guinea), and is played by rubbing the tops of the teeth with a moist or rosined hand. Each tooth rings briefly.

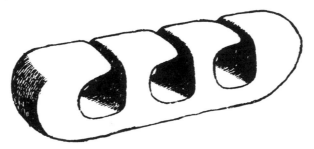

Figure 70. *'Nunut'*

My understanding of the instrument came when I had a chance to play one in the Folk Museum in Rotterdam. I first of all made some experiments in wood and bamboo (figures 71 and 72) and then decided to use glazed pottery (figure 73). I could then use water when stroking the teeth, and the sound lasted longer. I used a gourd to amplify the sound. (The gourd is used as a resonator in the North Indian 'vina' (figure 74).)

Figure 71. *Wood*

Figure 72. *Bamboo*

Figure 73. *Clay*

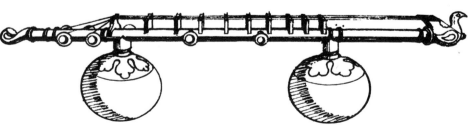

Figure 74. *North Indian 'vina'*

It was a logical step to follow this design with one in steel, and to have it plated with chromium. The tuning of this example is a whole tone scale ascending from middle C. Each tongue is graded in length, but the top two tongues, although different in length, give the same note. I found this same phenomenon with both the ceramic and wooden versions.

The resonator is resined canvas and the stand is Dexion 'Speed-frame' (square-section metal tube). When playing with two hands, a continuous sound is possible.

Playing together

This section is for group leaders, that is, people who can keep time. The structures I have notated below are just the bare bones. Accents and choice of notes can be immediate additions to the sound texture; other qualities may develop through players improvising within the structure as they gain confidence in their playing roles. It is worth while recording the music, so that everyone can hear how the sounds mesh, and how each performer's playing figures in the texture.

The foundation of my system is a regular pulse. This is represented by the vertical lines of the grid. The horizontal lines represent players, and the dots are the beats to play on.

The first structure (figure 75) is the one I referred to at the beginning of the book. Players choose a number between one and six.

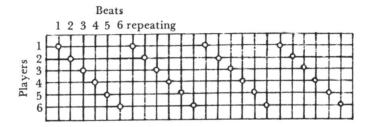

Figure 75. *First structure*

When their number is called, they play a single note. It is essential for someone to count out loud to begin with, but as players feel the pulse, the counting can be dropped. This first structure implies that whatever size the group is all the numbers have been chosen. It is of course feasible that everyone may choose beat 1 to play on, leaving the rest silent.

The second structure (figure 76) requires that the group of players divide into two. Group 1 plays on beat one, in every two. Group 2

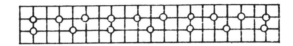

Figure 76. *Second structure*

plays on beat one in every three. This is a simple crossing pattern, that repeats every six beats.

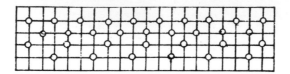

Figure 77. *Third structure*

For the third structure (figure 77) divide group 1 into two and give one half beat one, and the other half beat two in a two beat. Divide group 2, and give one half beat one and the other half beat three in a three beat. This will still repeat every six beats, but is more complex. These pieces have no natural ending, unless everyone starts together and stops after the structure has been repeated an agreed number of times, thus a sign from the conductor may prove the simplest way of stopping.

Some instruments, such as the tin fiddle, have a range of notes, others, such as the bamboo chime bar, are single-note instruments and would need to be grouped to increase the range; the two-flute has an assortment of sounds. Players can be allowed to improvise within their structures, to bring further colour to the sound. I would hope that the disciplines involved might gradually be relaxed, and players be sensitive to each others' sounds, so that a natural homogeneity will begin to prevail.

Roots and innovation – music in education

JOHN PAYNTER

Does music have a place in the curriculum? Certainly many people think it has. But having agreed thus far, the next question is rather more difficult. What is the proper *role* for music in schools?

Over the years we have been made particularly conscious of the ways in which music seems to have lagged behind the visual arts, English, dance and drama in education. We have been reminded too of the recipients' viewpoint: those pupils who found the traditional approaches to music 'useless and boring'.* Some of the problems are simply matters of history. Music entered the general curriculum of maintained secondary schools as part of the legacy of the older Public schools. There music had been principally a recreational, cultural 'extra' for the few, brought out and shown off to everyone on Founder's Day, Speech Day or some similar festival. That is a tradition not easily forgotten.

There have been other pressures — reactions, perhaps, to the Speech Day music ritual: attempts to give music standing in the eyes of colleagues and pupils by aligning it with 'respectable' information-based subjects. 'Knowing about' then becomes more important than 'experience of'. One way or the other, music remained the province of the gifted few. The idea that music could have a place in the education of *all* pupils was not to be taken seriously. The facts seemed self-evident; music was for musicians. Our ready willingness to accept such 'facts' has been bolstered by a tendency to under-value non-verbal means of expression. It has taken many years for us even to begin to glimpse the possibilities the arts offer in the education of sensitivity, imagination and inventiveness — what Robert Witkin has called 'the intelligence of feeling'. These are areas of possibly far greater importance than we recognise in our fast-moving modern industrial society.

However, a change of climate for music in education is gradually taking place. We are aware now that music can have relevance for many more people if it is approached by way of its own 'raw materials'. As a starting point, the sounds themselves make more impact than verbal information. In this context, a programme of sound-exploration can provide a strong basis for music sessions in schools and in colleges of higher education. Because such a programme

*Schools Council, *Enquiry 1, Young school leavers*, HMSO 1968; part II, chapter 3, § 85.

97

is not dependent upon a prescribed body of information but rather upon the inventiveness and imagination which each individual brings to the classroom, it characterises the changes we are now beginning to see in music education in schools; in particular, the movement away from over-emphasis upon *instruction* (the 'received wisdom'; the heritage of accepted and acceptable music techniques) and towards a new *educational* view of music for the majority. Skills are still vital, but only as and when they are needed: a preliminary to a particular line of experiment, or arising out of exploration. There will be a variety of activities and possibilities rather than a narrowly pre-ordered formula. While some activities will require an element of training, in general a new concept calls for a broader design than that which sufficed for a 'master and apprentice' relationship. If we really are going to offer opportunities for everyone to participate fruitfully, we shall have to recognise individual interests and accept that different starting points mean also a number of paths to be followed simultaneously. Obviously this is more difficult to handle as a class-teaching method, but a music 'workshop' can be an immensely rewarding experience for both pupil and teacher. 'Experiment' signifies a journey into unknown territory; the outcome cannot be known beforehand. Nevertheless, the teacher must not abandon his responsibility to teach. He must have a clear view of the possibilities and be ready with techniques and advice, whichever way the exploration leads. Neither must he be afraid to demonstrate or to offer help on the basis of his own experience and knowledge. Possibly the greatest danger, whenever we try to initiate new teaching methods, is that out of zeal for innovation we let go our roots.

Music is essentially a *sound* experience. It is both a way of listening to sounds and a way of organising experience in sound. Musical inventiveness starts with sound-sources — trying out different vocal effects; exploring the resonance of wood, metal, glass, stone or any other material. Having found the resources and tried them out, the next step is improvisation leading to repetition and the establishment of certain patterns which we find pleasing. This is musical composition. Unlike composition in some other materials — paint, for instance, or clay — music's greatest drawback is its intangible nature. The sounds are there for a few seconds, and then they are gone. So we must find ways of preserving the experience. Musical notations (there are many forms: it all depends on *what* you want to notate) provide retrieval systems for ideas and patterns in sound. But more fundamental is the definition of the sound-source: the designed musical 'instrument'. It is here that the tangible and the intangible meet.

A useful music course could be devised, for secondary school or college, around exploration of the sound properties of different materials. Start by exploring all the sounds in one room, classifying them by pitch (high, middle, low) or by quality/material (wood sounds, glass or metal). Which sounds can easily be sustained? Which objects produce only short sounds? Combine groups of sounds and experiment with textures. Then, with the whole-class group or with small groups suitably separated, organise improvisation sessions using what has been discovered. Work on some of the improvisations until they become compositions which can be notated in whatever way seems most appropriate for the sounds used, or simply preserved in tape recordings. If the work has been done in small groups, make sure time is allowed for the groups to 'share' finished pieces. Whenever music is made it should be performed. This is also an opportunity for the teacher to comment and encourage; a matter of importance if the work is to grow and have a sense of purpose.

From such beginnings it is a short step to gathering 'found objects', perhaps seeking out particular sound-qualities, and then arranging them to form 'instruments'. Encourage inventiveness and the imaginative use of sounding objects or components. Try to avoid the most obvious imitation of existing instruments, though there will be occasions when, quite properly, you may want to start from direct imitation and then allow for imagination to play with the possibilities of *development* or with the use of new materials for an old model. Great care will be needed in making, but equal care in devising. And do not despise the fantastic. There is no telling where ideas may lead.

Organisationally, a course on these lines will be most effective as an on-going 'workshop' rather than a series of traditionally arranged 'lessons' (and, as things develop, there will no doubt be need for actual workshop facilities — in the craft sense — for designing and building instruments; though it is surprising how much can be achieved with only makeshift arrangements). There are, frequently, opportunities for drawing together the arts in the curriculum, and although each area will, understandably, have reason to preserve its special interests as 'music', 'art', 'dance' or whatever, there can be strength and purposefulness in association wherever it seems appropriate. *Jointly* the arts educate the imagination and the feelings. It is a unique contribution to the educational process.

Exploring sonorities; inventing, designing and building new instruments — sometimes complex, sometimes very simple. There is so much music to be experienced in doing just that (incidentally, it is quite a good idea to encourage the group to build between them one large 'composite' instrument as well as developing individual ideas). But there would be no point in constructing instruments if they were not put to use. You may want to play well-known traditional pieces and there is nothing wrong with that if the instruments are suitable. But if the design has moved away from traditional forms, it would seem only natural to let the new instrumental shapes suggest new musical shapes. As soon as there are enough finished instruments to

99

make even a small ensemble, encourage the makers to play them, first improvising, paying particular attention to the special characteristics of each instrument, and then working up ideas into group compositions. And when several compositions have been made and remembered, everything else can stop for a concert.

There are any number of avenues to follow. If may seem sufficient to explore sounds, make instruments and create music. Certainly a worthwhile course could be made in that way. On the other hand, you may wish to go further and link with other aspects of music, and once again there are many possibilities.

Perhaps the most obvious links are with the historical development of musical instruments; drums, flutes, plucked strings, bowed strings, keyed instruments, and so on.* The same developments can be explored geographically: studying the instruments from cultures outside Europe may be a spur to invention when it comes to making our own 'new' instruments.

Then there are composers who — especially in the twentieth century — have extended the scope of music by constructing new apparatus for producing it. One of the most notable is the American, Harry Partch, who spent a lifetime investigating those tiny divisions of sound we call microtones and building instruments (some very large indeed: giant marimbas and huge glass bowls) which would encompass his new and extended scales — sometimes with as many as 43 tones to the octave. Although to some extent superseded by electronic sound synthesisers, there is nevertheless something very personal and fundamental about an instrument, unusual in construction, that has been designed and built, worked on carefully piece by piece, and then brought to life in music which reveals not only the instrument's potential but also its limitations. Perhaps the synthesiser is not sufficiently limited? When we hear a Mozart concerto played on a modern valve horn, we may easily forget the oddly 'out of tune' quality of the old hand-stopped 'natural' horn (Britten uses it for the opening and concluding sections for his *Serenade* for tenor, horn and strings), but that was the sound Mozart had in mind when he composed his concertos. The 'natural' instrument — warts and all — was part of the composition process; a thought which should encourage us to make the most of whatever oddities of sound our own invented instruments may possess.

It is important, in any study of the development of instruments and their use in music — European or otherwise; ancient or modern — that we *hear the music*. Recordings may not always be easy to find. Partch's music was originally recorded privately on a series known as *Gate 5*, though some pieces have now been issued commercially by the big companies. For ethnic musics there is no better collection

*A useful book is Curt Sachs, *The History of Musical Instruments*, Dent, 1968.

than the wide-ranging catalogue of the American Folkways label. But in addition to these somewhat specialised fields, there is a vast range of twentieth-century music, from rock to the 'serious' *avant-garde*, that exploits new sound techniques. In a course based on the exploration of sounds, there is a lot of food for thought and discussion in, say, the deliberately distorted, amplified sounds of the 'Rolling Stones'; the amazing variety of metal and glass sounds in Takemitsu's *Seasons for Percussion*; the constantly changing string textures of Penderecki's *Threnody*; or the strangely new but equally 'ancient' qualities of John Cage's music for 'prepared' piano (with all its associations with Indonesian gamelan music — another avenue to be explored).

It should, then, be possible to formulate a programme — perhaps a year's course, perhaps longer — on these principles; exploring, experimenting, inventing, constructing, creating music and performing, investigating developments historically and ethnically, hearing recordings (and occasional live performances) of music on new or rediscovered instruments or from other musical cultures. It would be a programme implying an 'open' attitude to music; one that might frequently lead away from the traditional topics we may hitherto have thought of as central to any music course. But if, by its essentially active and creative structure, it turned out to have wider appeal than traditionally organised courses, would that be such a bad thing?

Bibliography

BY JOHN PAYNTER

The following may be found helpful when it comes to making music with the instruments you have built:

Brian Dennis, *Experimental Music in Schools*, Oxford University Press, 1970.

Brian Dennis, *Projects in Sound*, Universal Edition, London, 1975

Harry Partch, *Genesis of a Music*, Da Capo Reprints, 1974.

John Paynter & Peter Aston, *Sound and Silence*, Cambridge University Press, 1970.

John Paynter, *Hear and Now*, Universal Edition, London, 1972.

Steve Reich, *Writings about Music*, Universal Edition, London, 1974.

R. Murray Schafer, *The Composer in the Classroom*, BMI Canada, 1965.*

R. Murray Schafer, *Ear Cleaning*, BMI Canada, 1965.*

R. Murray Schafer, *When Words Sing*, BMI Canada, 1970.*

R. Murray Schafer, *The Rhinoceros in the Classroom*, Universal Edition, London, 1975.

George Self, *New Sounds in Class*, Universal Edition, London, 1967.

George Self, *Make a New Sound*, Universal Edition, London, 1976.

David Toop (ed.), *New/Rediscovered Musical Instruments*, Quartz/Mirliton, London, 1974.

*Available in UK from Universal Edition (London) Ltd.

ADDITIONS SUGGESTED BY DAVID SAWYER

Alexander Buchner, *Folk Music Instruments of the World*, Octopus Books, 1973.

Sybil Marcuse, *Musical Instruments: A Comprehensive Dictionary*, Norton, New York, 1975.